**Rochdale
Libraries**
books and more...

Please return/renew this item
by the last date shown.
Books may also be renewed by
phone or via the web.

phone: 03003038876 or web
www.rochdale.gov.uk/libraries

BRITISH DOLLS
OF THE 1950s

Pedigree Saucy Walker

BRITISH DOLLS OF THE 1950s

SUSAN BREWER

REMEMBER WHEN

First published in Great Britain in 2009 by
REMEMBER WHEN
an imprint of
Pen & Sword Books Ltd
47 Church Street
Barnsley
South Yorkshire
S70 2AS

ISBN 978 1 84468 053 5

Printed and bound in Thailand
By Kyodo Nation Printing Services Co., Ltd

Pen & Sword Books Ltd incorporates the imprints of
Pen & Sword Aviation, Pen & Sword Maritime, Pen & Sword Military,
Wharncliffe Local History, Pen & Sword Select, Pen & Sword Military Classics,
Leo Cooper, Remember When, Seaforth Publishing and Frontline Publishing

For a complete list of Pen & Sword titles please contact
PEN & SWORD BOOKS LIMITED
47 Church Street, Barnsley, South Yorkshire, S70 2AS, England
E-mail: enquiries@pen-and-sword.co.uk
Website: www.pen-and-sword.co.uk

Contents

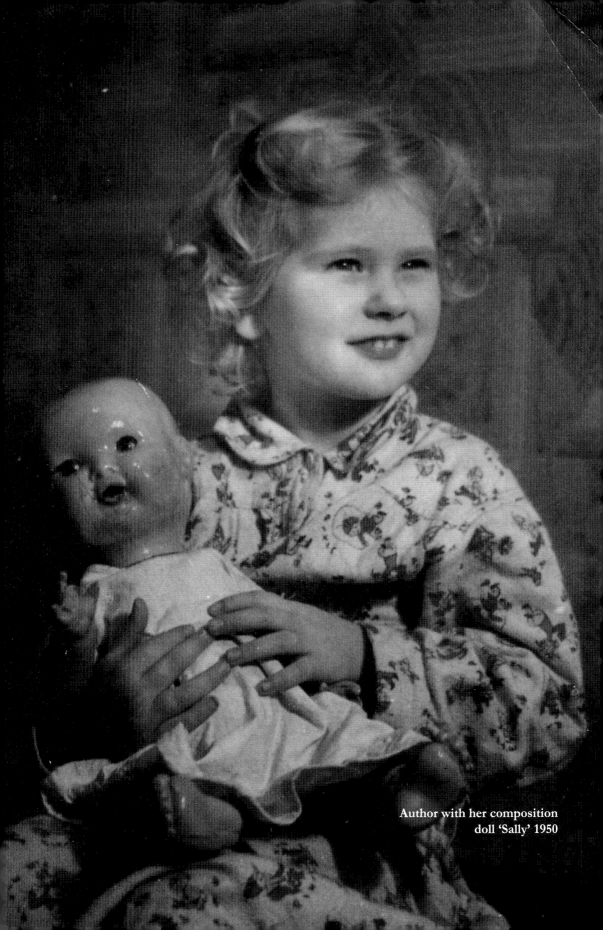

Author with her composition
doll 'Sally' 1950

Introduction

Why yet another doll book? Surely there are enough? How can there be so much to say about a simple doll?

But that's just it, there is a lot to say – every doll is different, the faces, the construction, the materials, the style. The history of the companies which made the dolls is intricate, interwoven with diverse personalities and obscure takeovers. Often, many of the records have been lost or destroyed, because the company believed that no-one would ever be interested. Consequently, I have painstakingly put together many details, especially relating to the smaller factories, from brief references gleaned from a variety of sources. However, I certainly don't profess to have included every 1950s doll here. Instead, I have selected some of my favourites from the hundreds of dolls which appeared during the decade, and I hope that amongst them are some of your favourites too.

This, though, is a more than just another doll book – this is an unashamed nostalgic wallow through post-war 1950s Britain. The decade began on rather a grey note before recovering its pride with the Festival of Britain, and recovering its pomp with the Coronation of Her Majesty Queen Elizabeth II. Colour, modern design, new inventions and crazy music were the hallmarks of the 1950s. Looking on were silent witnesses – the dolls of the era!

Susan Brewer

1950's Timeline

1950

The average UK annual salary was £101. *Palitoy* produced Pin-Up dolls. The majority of dolls were now made from hard plastic.

1951

Festival of Britain. A commemorative 'Amazing Miss Britain' doll issued.

1952

Accession of Queen Elizabeth II. *Rosebud* produced Miss Rosebud.

1953

Coronation. Many commemorative dolls produced by companies such as *Pedigree*, *Rosebud* and *Mark Payne*.

1954

Food rationing finally ended. *Philmar* registered their new line of paper dolls.

1955

Film 'Blackboard Jungle' began the teen cult with Rock Around the Clock. *Pedigree* issued a range of knee-jointed dolls.

1956

Elvis Presley entered the charts with 'Heartbreak Hotel'. *Palitoy* introduced their Petal Skin dolls.

1957

Launch of Sputnik. *Pedigree* produced Pretty Peepers and also dolls with rooted hair.

1958

Queen awarded Prince Charles the title of Prince of Wales. *Amanda Jane Company* introduced Jinx.

1959

The average UK salary had almost doubled since 1950. First Barbie doll produced in America, which later was to have a huge impact on British dolls. The majority of dolls were now made of softer vinyl.

Chapter 1

A Potted History of Dolls

As long as there have been children, there have been dolls. No doubt our earliest ancestors fashioned them from bone, skin and feathers. No one knows for certain just when the first doll was made. It is tempting to think of cave-dwelling children wrapping a stone in a scrap of fur and pretending it was a baby. Imagine a little Roman girl gouging a handful of clay from the river bank and roughly moulding it into the shape of a baby – it's quite possible. Think of an Indian child finding a pebble shaped rather like the human form, using dyes to paint eyes and a mouth upon the pebble's 'face.' Or an English child, centuries ago, carving facial features onto an apple found in an orchard, before ramming twigs into it to form a body. These creations might not resemble the dolls we know today – but to a child with few playthings, they would have provided hours of enjoyment.

What are Dolls Made From?

Little girls have always loved dolls, perhaps it is inbuilt into their nature, just as a boy will automatically veer towards weapons. Right from earliest times dolls would have been made as playthings,

Eighteenth Century wooden doll

from any material the parents happened to have at hand. A bundle of rags, features crudely marked with a few stitches; a bunch of corn or grass, folded and tied; a lovingly carved piece of wood or maybe a couple of bones lashed together with a leather thong. Certainly, rag dolls were played with by early Egyptian children, and it is quite conceivable that many of the ancient clay figures, found by archaeologists in sites all over the world, could have been toys.

All kinds of materials have been pressed into service – the Americans have a tradition of using dried, pickled apples as dolls' heads, and English pedlars were sometimes made with walnut shell faces. Dolls have even been made from crab shells, sea shells and shoes. In times past, when money wasn't always forthcoming for toys, parents would dress up wooden spoons, paint faces on saucepans, and weave corn husks. Remember the little girl, Johnny, in *What Katy Did* by Susan Coolidge? Her beloved 'doll' was actually a small chair with an apron tied around it. She used to feed it 'medicine'! Dolls are still made of strange things today - doll artists strive to be different, to make original dolls which stand out amongst the millions of shop-bought playthings.

Wax doll 1900s

We Grow More Sophisticated

As people grew more sophisticated, dolls were made, not only to sell or to barter, but to use in theatrical performances, often as puppets. In Sixteenth Century Britain, papier mâché puppets were used to perform plays or tales from the scriptures; the actors who provided the voices, told the story and played the music, would travel with their puppets around the country, attracting large crowds wherever they went.

Many small carved wooden dolls were sold at fairs, but they weren't called 'dolls' then - the cry was 'Come, buy my pretty babies'! Most probably these dolls were whittled by the vendors themselves, or their friends and families, and hawked around the villages. Doll production began in earnest during the Seventeenth Century, when larger heavy wooden dolls appeared. Nowadays, these dolls, with their serene expressions and dark glass eyes (with no pupils), are often referred to as 'Queen Anne Dolls' and change hands for enormous sums of money.

Later came dolls made from wax, which gave them beautiful translucent faces. Wax was quite a good medium for dolls because it felt soft and warm to the touch. It was malleable and could also be poured into a mould. It did, however, melt, chip and crack, and no doubt many little girls suffered great trauma when, after a game in the sun with their dolls, they returned to find a shapeless mass of molten wax.

Some of the makers of these wax dolls painstakingly used a hot needle to insert strands of human hair into the doll's head, one hair at a time. It must have taken a tremendous amount of patience, and not surprisingly, these wax dolls were very costly, and only the rich could afford them. Poorer children made do with little carved wooden dolls, known as 'Dutch dolls', or 'Penny Woodens', or had paper dolls which were printed onto flat sheets ready to be cut out at home. Wooden dolls were popular right up until the early decades of the Twentieth Century. Companies such as *Dean's Rag Books* sold calico sheets printed with the back and front of a doll, ready to be cut out and stuffed at home.

China

Bisque china dolls were popular during the Nineteenth and early Twentieth Century and when they were introduced, children – with rich parents – must have been thrilled. In fact, many were sold as 'fashion dolls' to ladies, and were never intended for children at all. Some of these dolls were exquisite, with delicate colouring, lifelike glass eyes and beautiful human-hair wigs. Occasionally the bodies, too, were made from china, but more often they were created from kid leather stuffed with sawdust, or made from a mixture of glue, plaster and sawdust known as 'composition'. These composition bodies eventually ousted the leather type, because they could be fitted with ball and socket joints which meant the dolls could assume lifelike poses.

The matt finish of the bisque gave the dolls' faces a silky sheen, a lustre which made them look almost real. Bisque has a smooth feel and delicate look. Today, French-made dolls, such as those by *Bru* and *Jumeau*, command exceptionally high prices: then, as now, the

Collection of bisque dolls 1900-1920s

German-made dolls were often more affordable. The Germans were skilled at mass-marketing, and gradually the French doll designers found they were unable to compete.

Most little Edwardian girls would have a special, favourite doll – probably German - which they would proudly take for walks in their high-sided leather perambulators and, except during the war years of 1914-1918, German bisque dolls cornered the market right up until the second world war. At first dolls were made to resemble adults or older children but gradually baby and toddler styles developed. When bent-limbed baby dolls were introduced in the early 1900s they became extremely popular; after all, most small girls wanted a 'baby' of their own, and by the late 1920s the *Armand Marseille* 'Dream Baby' was to be found in many little girl's homes.

Cloth, Celluloid, Composition

Now that doll making was big business, manufacturers experimented with many other materials – rubber (which flaked and discoloured), celluloid (highly inflammable), composition (cracked or crazed badly) and even metal (cold to touch and dented easily) - in order to find the perfect doll. In the first half of the Twentieth Century, cloth dolls became very popular, sometimes with papier mâché heads, but more often with faces made from pressed felt or stiffened buckram. Companies including *Chad Valley* and *Dean's and Norah Wellings* produced thousands of fabric dolls. Some of these were really lovely, but the main drawbacks were that they couldn't be bathed: moths liked the taste and the dolls tended to slowly disintegrate with all the loving hugs. Cloth dolls, though, have always had a place in children's

Composition doll 1940s

hearts, and are especially ideal for toddlers as they are light and soft. Most modern cloth dolls can be washed.

In the 1930s, many of the bisque manufacturers switched to composition and some lovely dolls were made completely of the substance. It was much cheaper to produce than bisque, and could also be made as a 'cottage industry' product (as a kiln and clay were unnecessary). Composition dolls had a more homely appearance and were quite robust, though did have a tendency to craze and could still smash if dropped. Gradually composition took over from bisque, and most 1930s and 1940s dolls were of this type. In fact, composition dolls were still being sold in Britain in the mid-1950s.

Doll Hospitals

Although it's hard to imagine now, most towns during the heyday of doll production sported a doll hospital, where children could bring their broken dolls, and leave them to be repaired or rewigged. Some of these hospitals were tiny shops tucked away up a side street, but some were huge: stocking not only new parts for broken dolls, but also outfits, prams, cots and hundreds of other accessories. Normally, the child took the doll to the hospital for 'treatment', collecting it as good as new after a few days. Replacement limbs, wigs, eyes or even new heads could be purchased; many a small girl must have been amazed when, after handing in a sad-faced doll with a cracked head, she was presented with a mended doll beaming from ear to ear!

Of course, when plastic was invented, the doll scene changed dramatically. Not only were dolls almost unbreakable, they were cheap to produce, which meant that instead of a little girl having just one or two dolls, she could have lots. As it became apparent that a broken plastic doll would just be thrown out with the rubbish rather than be taken to be lovingly restored, the Doll Hospitals virtually disappeared, however there are still a few to be found dotted around the country.

The Plastic Revolution

The Second World War ended in 1945, and toy companies were keen to utilise the modern plastics which they had been using throughout the war, in munitions work, into their peacetime products. However, they didn't all change immediately – for one thing, moulds and machinery were expensive, and needed to be sourced. Composition dolls were still in vogue during the early years of the 1950s, though by the end of the decade they were virtually obsolete, due to the rapid strides made in the plastics industries. Once plastic had arrived, both children and parents realised that it was far superior to composition, as it was lightweight and less likely to crack or chip.

By 1950, toys were filling the shops again, though not everything was easy to replace. There were still shortages, and for many, money was still tight. Small, cheap dolls, however, were bestsellers – they could be bought for pennies from toy shops and stores such as Woolworths. Though nowadays we tend to think of them as 'dolls house dolls' they were, at the time, a very real alternative to larger dolls for thousands of children. Swathed in crepe paper, scraps of fabric or tiny knitted dresses, these dolls were ideal for playing schools, shops or hospitals; they could be incorporated into matchboxes, tobacco tins or even nutshells, according to the size of the doll. Shoe boxes, too, were useful to make into schools; lack of toys and

Set of small dolls by Codeg

money meant that children's creative abilities were exercised to the full in the 1950s.

These tiny dolls, from makers such as *Kleeware*, *Sarold*, *Palitoy* and *Rodnoid*, were often moulded all in one piece, frequently in a sitting position, or were simply strung with a thread or thin 'shirring' elastic. They could be bought singly, or, in the case of the very tiny dolls, bought as a boxed set, such as one containing three rubbery babies. The box bore the description, 'They will stand up, they will sit down, clap their hands, kiss their toes,' which would never pass today's Trades Description Act, as in fact the dolls don't really do anything at all! The box seems to indicate it contains something quite exciting, but actually, each $1^1/2$ inch high baby is unjointed and is modelled in a seated position. These dolls were labelled as a *Codeg* production, Made in England.

Often found are small, 4 inch high, hard plastic dolls marked *Palitoy*, with elasticated joints and sleep eyes. Sometimes these are bald-headed, and other times have wisps of mohair as 'wigs'. They have distinctive pointing fingers on their left hands and were sold either naked or wearing a basic cotton dress. Sometimes these inexpensive novelties were packed in little wicker or cardboard cribs from stores such as Woolworths.

Small Palitoy dolls

Many of the dolls in the late 1940s and very early 1950s were made from pre-war moulds. Companies which were now experimenting with plastics continued to use the moulds previously used to produce dolls made from composition, as they all wanted to be amongst the first to get their new, plastic dolls into the shops. At this time, however, composition was still being used for doll making, as was celluloid and rubber – it was expensive to change to the equipment needed to make plastic, so many companies decided to forgo the expense and continue as they had been doing. Other companies, though already making plastic, continued producing their earlier dolls too.

Some companies embraced the new plastic with such glee that they embarked on all kinds of domestic items, from combs to cups, buttons to bangles. They also made toys of all kinds, so dolls became a mere sideline – though today doll collectors tend to assume that the dolls were the most important item of all, in reality they were only a small part of the overall production.

Author's childhood dolls

By the early 1950s, immigrants, especially from the West Indies, were becoming a common sight in many towns. They were recruited to help with our decreased labour force and because these people had children, they needed dolls. Many companies produced black dolls, either using existing moulds – so the dolls were black skinned with Caucasian features – or using new moulds with West Indian features, to make the dolls more realistic. Sometimes these dolls had black, curly astrakhan wigs, and sometimes the curls were moulded into the plastic. Every little girl in the 1950s wanted a black doll to enhance her collection.

Though the 1950s began with many people still poor, or with little spare cash, things improved throughout the decade – by the end of it, living standards were much higher. It was reckoned that by the early 1950s, the days of cheap and shoddy – but expensive – wartime toys were over: Christmas 1952 promised to the best since the 1930s. The larger department stores were revitalised and John Lewis mounted a Christmas Toy Fair which displayed a wider choice of toys than had been seen since 1945.

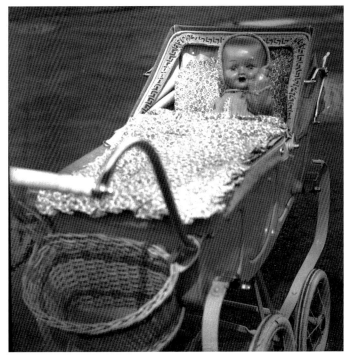

Author's composition doll in her Dunkley pram

Chapter 2

The Colour Returns

Britain in 1951 was still suffering from the aftermath of the war – many goods were on ration, bomb sites scarred the streets, and people were trying to rebuild shattered lives. The country needed cheering up; an assurance that good times were just around the corner. The Festival of Britain helped to dispel some of our post-war gloom. Then came the coronation – and after that, the face of Britain changed. We were into new 'Elizabethan' era – new discoveries, new fashions, new music, new lifestyles, and, of course, new dolls.

Like a land waking from a long sleep, Britain became revitalised. At the start of the decade, most streets, especially in London and other large towns and cities, sported bomb sites – heaps of rubble overgrown with weeds and yellow ragwort. These were cleared and new buildings appeared, often tall blocks of flats which initially seemed the answer to the housing shortage, but soon developed problems of their own, notably leaving many of the tenants, especially the elderly, with a feeling of isolation.

However, we didn't know this at the time, we just marvelled at the way the country was being transformed. Everything was affected, from ceramics, art, fashion, music and food, to transport, medicine, communications and industry. New discoveries and inventions were constantly in the news, and by the end of the decade the space race was in full spate. Children, especially, followed developments closely, intrigued by Sputniks and dog-carrying space capsules. The 1950s was an exciting period, and a time of rapid change.

Festival and Coronation

At last there was a light on the horizon, and shops which had been so bare for so long were beginning to stock exciting products again. Amongst them were toys. Initially there was such a huge demand (once the war ended in 1945, soldiers returned to their wives and babies were the order of the day!) that it was often necessary to search long and hard for certain items. Also, many of the earliest post-war produced toys were mainly made for export. My parents wanted to buy me a doll's pram in 1951 for my fourth birthday, and apparently it took a great deal of hunting before the desired pram was found. It had been worth waiting for, though. My pram was a pale grey coach-built *Dunkley*, to replace the little red *Tri-ang* tin pram I had grown out of. I pushed that pram with its passengers of a composition doll and a teddy bear for miles. Along pavements, through parks and even to school – my *Dunkley* and I were welded together! (See Chapter 8.)

Festival Of Britain

In 1951, as a not-quite-four year old, I remember standing on Westminster bridge with my Dad. It was night-time, and he had brought me to this part of London, from our home in Brixton, to

Author's father took this photo of the Skylon when they saw 'the marvellous sight'

show me a marvellous sight; there, lighting up the night sky was a clear, white, tapered cylinder. 'That's called the Skylon,' said Dad, 'And it's part of the Festival of Britain.'

Of course, I didn't know then what a 'Festival of Britain' was, but I did know that it must be special to have a beautiful, glowing light in the sky. When the Festival opened, the Skylon towered above the event; a graceful, 300ft tall futuristic piece of engineering, made from aluminium and steel, with no visible means of support. Many years later I learned that the Festival was opened on May 3rd by King George VI and Queen Elizabeth (later to become the Queen Mother), and it was a celebration of all that was new in British design; a kind of antidote to the depression and drabness which followed in the aftermath of the Second World War. It was to commemorate the centenary of the Great Exhibition of 1851, which had been inaugurated by Prince Albert and took place in a magnificent crystal palace.

The 1951 event took place on Southbank, alongside the River Thames, in the heart of London, an area of marshy ground which was gradually being reclaimed from the river. This 'Festival of Britain' was an attempt to show the British public - and in fact, the world - that Britain was getting back onto its feet, with British industry booming once more and British culture thriving. Purpose built exhibition pavilions were erected, covering a wide range of topics including Health, Sport, The Country, Transport, Sea and Ships, Sky, Land, Polar, Outer Space, New Schools, People of Britain, Television, Living World, Power and Production and The Natural Scene.

Guidebook to the Festival of Britain

Festival Doll

One of the souvenirs sold at the Festival of Britain was a little doll. This doll, though perhaps not much to look at, provided a great deal of amusement for both children and adults. She was a novelty doll – she could walk, dance or even hop!

Sold in a paper packet, labelled 'The Amazing Miss Britain of 1951, A Souvenir of the Royal Festival Gardens', the blurb boasted, 'She will jive and dance to your radio, piano or gramophone, and obey your every command! Guaranteed to work and absolutely foolproof'. The doll was made out of card, and resembled a glamorous, curvy blonde wearing a red ribbon trimmed bra, matching panties with criss-crossed fastenings (quite risqué for the time), red peep-toe sandals, a red bracelet and sparkly earrings – the clothes were all printed onto the card. She was actually fashioned from nine separate pieces of card, all cleverly riveted together so that her joints were mobile.

The comprehensive instructions read:

INSTRUCTIONS

Please read these carefully before attempting to work the Model. You have been amused and intrigued by this fascinating little novelty. You too can baffle and entertain your friends so long as you keep the secret, which, as in all good tricks, is very simple. The Model is supported by the cardboard tab at the back of its head, by a long length of thin cotton, thread or nylon stocking thread which should be of a colour to match the background where you wish the Model to perform. Keep your friends a few feet away and then the thread will be quite invisible to them.

Rare Festival of Britain doll

Tie the thread to a drawing pin behind the leg of a chair, at a height of 2 or 3 inches behind the Model's head. Carry the thread across to another chair or table leg at a distance of about 3 to 4 feet away, where it should be placed around the leg or through a screw eye and these should be as far as possible from the person operating it. The thread must be pulled tight to allow the Model to stand up and tugged gently till she dances.

The explanation of the demonstration which you have just witnessed is that the Model has been worked by an extended movement. If you then hide a friend behind your chair or any large piece of furniture, the effect will be perfect. Failing this he may sit with the other people who are watching you and the model. It is of course quite possible for you to do it yourself but [this] has the disadvantage of not allowing you complete freedom of movement. The pulling should be done as far away as possible from where the friend is hiding.

The thread may be taken all round the room if necessary, using the legs of furniture or small screw eyes for the purpose. The model is NOT FIXED to the thread. It simply hangs like washing on a clothes line. Play your radio for it to dance to – it's a lot more fun. Cover the tag with your fingers when showing your friend the back of the Model.

Don't tell your friends how it is done. So long as you keep the secret, the trick is always good for a repeat performance – but as in all conjuring tricks and stage illusions, it will lose its appeal once the secret is known.

Rare Festival of Britain doll packet

This little cardboard 'Model' as she was referred to, must have given plenty of amusement at the time, but being so fragile, it is unsurprising that she is a rare find today.

The Coronation

The Coronation meant celebration, and as the big day approached – June 2nd 1953 – bunting, flags and souvenirs began to appear in the shops. Mugs and jugs bearing the new Queen's likeness appeared, as did pens, badges, scarves and puzzles. And, of course, commemorative dolls appeared. Some of these dolls were intended as souvenirs, often for adults, while others were 'representations' of a queen, often just a basic doll dressed in queenly attire. Most of these were intended for children and many were dressed by mums, grans and aunties.

Coronation Day itself was marked by street parties throughout Britain – practically every street in Britain was lined with trestle tables, heaped with sandwiches, cakes and jellies. The whole country was celebrating, and the streets were thronged with young and old, from tiny babies carried in their mother's arms to frail elderly folk who sat on bentwood chairs with cups of tea. Lamp posts were decorated with streamers, union jacks fluttered from windows, impromptu concerts broke out as mouth organs and squeeze-boxes were produced, and people danced along the pavements. I recall a large gold cardboard EIIR insignia which my parents hung from the window of our upstairs flat in Brixton. We had a fancy dress party in our street – I was a fairy, my older cousin, Raymond, was a golly, and my younger, Derek, was 'The Little Red Monkey' after a popular song of the time. My older cousin won, and received a soldier's outfit made from crepe paper and silver card as a prize.

Earlier, I had been one of the fortunate children able to watch the ceremony on television. My uncle and aunt, who lived quite near, had a television set with a tiny, flickering greeny-grey screen. My uncle had assembled it himself, and it was an extremely dangerous thing,

'In a Golden Coach' sheet music

with no protective glass over the screen, and loose wires sticking from the back. Lots of us gathered to watch, and my aunt, who was a dressmaker, had dressed a doll for me in a white satin gown and a magnificent purple velvet cloak. As I saw the Queen being crowned by the Archbishop of Canterbury, I reverently placed a cardboard crown on my Queen's head.

It was estimated that three million people lined London's streets to catch a glimpse of the new Queen as she travelled to and from Buckingham Palace, in the magnificent, gleaming golden state coach which was pulled by eight Windsor Greys. Many of the watchers had been camping overnight, determined to obtain a prime position from which to view the procession. Typically, even though it was the beginning of summer, it was pouring with rain, but the crowd's enthusiasm wasn't dampened – they cheered all the guests on their way to the Abbey. The horse-drawn coaches carried members of the Royal Family: visiting heads of state and representatives of Commonwealth countries. Queen Salote of Tonga, smiling through the rain in an open landau, proved a huge hit with the crowds.

When the Queen arrived at Westminster Abbey, she was wearing crimson velvet robes trimmed with ermine and bordered with gold lace, and on her head was a diamond diadem. Her beautiful Coronation gown incorporated all the floral symbols of the UK and

Coronation souvenirs

Commonwealth. This had been designed by Norman Hartnell after lengthy discussions with Her Majesty over the choice of style, and, especially, the embroidery details.

Once she had been acknowledged by all four corners of the Abbey, the Queen made her Coronation Oath. In this central, sacred act, the Maids of Honour removed the Queen's rich robes and opulent jewels, leaving her in a simple linen overdress. Dr Geoffrey Fisher, the Archbishop of Canterbury, then anointed the Queen with the holy oil, screened by a canopy. After the golden robes of the Supertunica were placed upon her, she took her place on King Edward's chair, above the Stone of Scone.

She was handed the symbols of authority; the sceptre, the orb, the rod of mercy and the royal sapphire and ruby ring. Finally, the Archbishop of Canterbury placed St Edward's Crown on her head to complete the ceremony. There was a cry of 'God Save the Queen', gun salutes were fired as crowds cheered, and all the nobility in the Abbey placed their coronets upon their heads. The young Prince

Charles watched as his mother was crowned, but, to her annoyance, Princess Anne had been deemed too young to attend the ceremony.

The ceremony was watched by millions of television viewers around the world, and the BBC set up their biggest ever outside broadcast which provided live coverage of the event on both radio and television. Later, the crowds outside Buckingham Palace watched as the Queen and other members of the Royal Family made six appearances on the balcony to greet the people and also to watch the Royal Airforce flypast. That evening, the Queen made a radio broadcast to thank people for their support throughout the day. She pledged, 'Throughout all my life and with all my heart I shall strive to be worthy of your trust'.

Coronation Dolls

In 1953, a lady called Peggy Nisbet, originally a designer at Bristol Pottery, decided to commemorate the Coronation with a model of the Queen. Her novel idea was to create a bisque figurine wearing a long gown, and then to fashion an outfit from silk and velvet to fit over the bisque, producing a cross between an ornament and a doll. Peggy decided to take her prototype to Harrods, and was amazed to gain an order for 250 dolls. She then had to hastily search for an artist to paint the faces and also for top-quality needle-women to sew the dresses. Working from home, Peggy somehow managed to get all the dolls assembled and delivered to Harrods in time for the Coronation. The dolls proved a great success, yet amazingly, in 1984 when the *Nisbet* company tried to find an example, they were unable to find a complete one, in spite of offering a reward. The only person who came forward with an original Coronation doll was an American lady, and her doll, which had the robe and crown, was missing the silk dress, orb and sceptre. Later, a replica porcelain doll was produced.

Peggy was so inspired by the initial success of her Coronation figures, that she decided to make further dolls, dressed in royalty-themed outfits. She aimed to use plastic rather than porcelain so that

A Peggy Nisbet Model
P1953
Replica Edition of
The First Nisbet Doll
Made in England

Nisbet reproduction of the original porcelain coronation doll

the dolls could be sold more cheaply. At first, she experimented with small dolls from companies such as *Rosebud*, finally producing a selection of beautifully-dressed dolls representing characters including Queen Elizabeth I, Henry VIII and Anne Boleyn. The main drawback with these was that they had childish faces, and Peggy wanted a more adult look to her dolls, as they were aimed at the souvenir market. Eventually, Peggy succeeded in getting her own design produced in a solid, matt-finish compound, much heavier than the plastic dolls of the time. It wasn't completely straightforward, and there were many problems encountered along

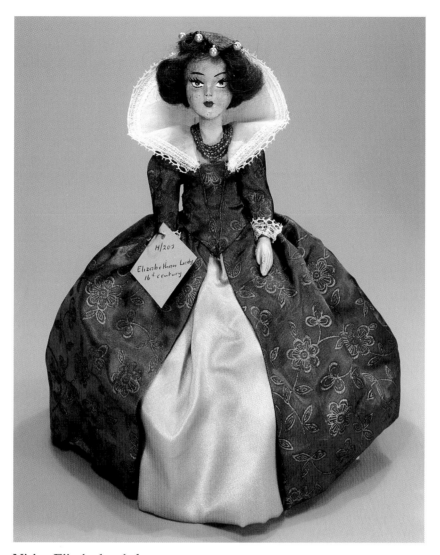

Nisbet Elizabethan lady

the way, such as unstable resin mixes, as well as problems with Henry VIII, whose fat tummy collapsed during the moulding process. The dolls needed to be solid, as the brocades and velvets which Peggy planned on using would not hang correctly on lightweight figures such as the *Rosebud* dolls she had previously used.

Collector Wendy Moorhen, from Berkshire, says that her true love of dolls began with the ones you don't play with; her father, who

Nisbet Henry VIII with some of his wives

worked in an Italian restaurant in Kensington, London, gave her an
Italian doll sourced from one of his colleagues, as a Christmas gift.
Wendy can still visualise her; she was small and her skirt was made
from orange velvety-type material with blue trimmings. Several other
foreign dolls followed but the 'control freak' in her longed for a
compatible series of dolls and thus began her lifelong interest in *Peggy
Nisbet* dolls. The first was an Eighteenth Century lady, dressed in a
pink brocade bodice and overskirt with a cream satin petticoat, the
bodice trimmed with a delicate lace. She was followed with Henry
VIII and two of his wives, Anne Boleyn and Anne of Cleves; Wendy
still believes these early models were some of the best ever produced.
The Can-Can dancer followed, embarrassing her with the saucy lace
knickers, fishnet stockings and garter. She was bought for the
princely sum of 29s. (that's £1.45 in today's money). Wendy saved
from her own pocket money, and her next acquisition was the
Fotheringhay costumed Mary Queen of Scots, bought from a store
on Princes Street in Edinburgh (though most of her dolls were
bought from Selfridges). She can recall a competition that was held,
the prize being a number of minutes in Selfridges let loose with a

Dean's 1953 Coronation Supplement

trolley to fill. Wendy adds that she was so excited imagining how she would spend all those precious minutes picking up *Peggy Nisbet* dolls and *Tri-ang* trains. Not winning was an early lesson that we don't get everything in life that we want!

The small but substantial dolls produced by Peggy's company measured between 7 to 8 inches tall, though size varied according to range. Each doll had hand-painted features and wore a detailed costume, which was carefully sewn to a high standard. The dolls could be broadly arranged by categories; Historical, British Traditional, Portrait, Shakespeare, National and Happy Dolls. In addition, there were limited editions, porcelain dolls, large vinyl dolls both for collectors and for 'play dolls', cloth dolls, teddy bears and soft toys. For around 30 years, Peggy reigned supreme as a designer of costume dolls, presiding over a huge concern, with factories and workshops in Weston-super-Mare and Scotland.

Dean's Ragbook company, which was established in 1903, issued a range of soft dolls and toys for the coronation. One collection was known as Coronation Cuddlums, and consisted of 'dolls in traditional colours for the very young'. These dolls had plush bodies and moulded faces, and were red or blue with white trims – very patriotic. Another doll, known as Cora-nation, was dressed in a clown-type red/white/blue outfit and pointed hat. The doll's smaller sibling was a Pierrot in similar colours. In addition, the company produced some soft bodied guardsmen, policemen and beefeaters, advertised as 'three musts for coronation year – souvenirs of a memorable occasion.'

Pedigree Toys dressed some of their small Delite characters as souvenirs of the great day, too. These included 7 inch twins Peer and Peeress, a 14 inch Peeress 'in approved Robes and Cap of State' and a 19 inch Marchioness 'beautifully robed, complete with jewelled tiara and coronet', all dressed ready for the coronation. Probably their biggest success was the Little Princess, a hard plastic play doll with a cheeky smile and a mass of curly hair, obviously based on the toddler Princess Anne.

An In-Depth Look at a Pedigree Little Princess

A pretty doll, standing 14 inches tall, she was made from hard plastic and featured an open smiling mouth revealing two upper teeth, and blue eyes which closed when she was laid down. Her lips were bright red, her cheeks flushed pink and her blonde wig was mohair with plenty of soft curls. She wore a cheeky look and bore more than a passing resemblance to the young Princess Anne; today this doll is a favourite with collectors.

The Little Princess was a sturdy, straight-legged doll, with dimpled knees. Both the knees and the hands were blushed, the hands being particularly well-modelled with splayed fingers (the standard *Pedigree* toddler hand.) The doll's back was marked 'Pedigree Made in England' and contained a 'mama' unit with a grid. Her neck was also marked *Pedigree*.

Little Princess by Pedigree
blue variation

Little Princess by Pedigree

Although *Pedigree* didn't actually claim that their doll was meant to be Anne, there were several clues. Apart from the likeness and the 'Little Princess' name, the box, a deep pink, featured a picture of the doll outside Buckingham Palace. In addition, the doll's outfit was designed by no less than Royal dress designer Norman Hartnell, who designed so many fabulous outfits for the Queen. *Pedigree* listed the doll in their standard 14SW range, but only briefly described her, saying her dress is 'beautiful'.

Little Princess was sold in a spotted white sleeveless taffeta dress. The spots were about pin-head sized, and were usually red or blue, though other colours have been found. Over the top of the dress was a delicate muslin overskirt, and the bodice featured a deep triangular-shaped collar. Both collar and overskirt were trimmed with lace and ric-rac braid. The dress bore a standard blue and white *Pedigree*-embroidered label on the back seam, and it fastened with two metal studs.

Underneath her dress Little Princess wore an all-in-one silk-look white nylon garment, which was edged around the legs with lace and tied at the neck with a fine crochet cord. Her white socks were the fishnet type and her white shoes tied with ribbon. Tie-ins with *Bestway* and with *Woman's Illustrated* magazine ensured additional sewing and knitting patterns. Other Hartnell designs for the doll – 'My Royal Wardrobe' – included 'My Coronation Robe of State', 'My Striped Frock', 'My Long Party Frock' and 'My Short Party Frock'. The Parisienne designer Pierre Balmain was responsible for her 'My Paris Wardrobe'. Amongst his outfits for the Little Princess doll were 'My Pretty Coat', 'My Balmain Party Frock' and 'My Middy Suit.' Each pattern cost around 1/3d (7p).

Norman Hartnell was born in London in 1901, and by the late thirties was dressmaker to the Royal Family, One of his most memorable collections was a stunning 'white wardrobe' produced for Queen Elizabeth (later the Queen Mother), which she wore on a state visit to Paris in 1938 whilst in mourning for her mother. Hartnell had to quickly change the ready-designed coloured garments, as black was considered unsuitable for a high summer collection to a fashionable country on the occasion of a friendly visit, he suggested white instead. It wowed the Parisians. He also designed the wedding dress and the Coronation gown for Queen Elizabeth II.

Pierre Balmain, born in 1914 in the Savoy district, south-east France, opened his Paris Haute Couture house in 1945 immediately after the war. His svelte tailored suits and elegant evening gowns became very fashionable, but later he moved from the world of couture to that of Hollywood, designing costumes for many famous film stars.

Other Pedigree Royal Dolls

Pedigree introduced other dolls with Royal connections too, notably Elizabeth. Elizabeth was a slim teen, standing 19 inches tall, and she originally cost 42/- (£2.10p). She was described in the 1953 *Pedigree* catalogue as having a 'Print Dress and Best Brushable Wig'. Her fair mohair – later saran – wig was quite short and waved, her slightly smiling mouth was closed, and she had flirty sleep eyes with black hair eyelashes. The plastic used in her construction was glossy and very smooth.

There were various patterns available, designed by Veronica Scott, the fashion editor of *Woman* magazine, to enable the budding young needle-woman to create a wardrobe of outfits for her. Although the doll didn't, in shape or form, resemble Her Majesty Queen Elizabeth II, the company must have boosted sales enormously just by giving the doll a queenly name. Amongst the patterns were dresses, beach wear, a duster coat, winter coat, underwear and nightdress, but they were quite complicated, and not really suitable for beginners in needlework.

Elizabeth by Pedigree

Elizabeth by Pedigree

Elizabeth was sold wearing a full-skirted cotton dress, in a choice of several designs and colours, featuring a distinctive large white petersham collar and a white belt. Her shoes had ribbon ties, she had short white socks and came in a pink and white striped box. This box bore an attractive drawing of Elizabeth in a blue patterned dress, and the advertising slogans included such comments as 'With all you need to dress her like a queen' and 'Sleeping and flirting eyes: skin smooth as silk'.

Slightly later, they issued a 14 inch Bonnie Charlie doll, which might or might not have been intended to tie-

Bonnie Charlie by Pedigree

in with the royal event. Bonnie Charlie was cute, with moulded hair and a shy smile. He wore a kilt, a white shirt and a sporran – very much like an outfit sometimes sported by the young Prince Charles.

Additional Royal Dolls

Naturally, many other companies issued Royal dolls – everyone wanted to cash in on the enormous wave of patriotism, as well as the great souvenir opportunity. Manufacturers such as *Rosebud* and *Roddy* produced dolls dressed as the Queen, while thousands of other dolls up and down the land were dressed in white gowns, velvet cloaks and crowns, or in suitably patriotic red, white and blue outfits by people working at home, to commemorate the event.

As I recounted earlier, my aunt had given me a doll which she had dressed as the Queen, and a cardboard crown to place on her head when the grand moment came. She had also dressed a larger doll in coronation robes to be exhibited in the window of the local dressmaking shop, in Clapham, where

Miss Rosebud as the Queen

Rosebud dolls dressed as coronation souvenirs using a 1953 *Woman's Weekly* pattern

she was employed as a 'piece worker' making clothes at home. Although I no longer have my Queen doll, I do have in my collection a *Roddy* doll which someone has painstakingly dressed in a white frock embroidered with the Queen's initials and date. The magazine *Woman's Weekly* also published a pattern to turn its little Rosebud twins into countesses (See Chapter 8).

The Coronation wasn't just celebrated here in Britain; countries across the globe rejoiced too. In America, Jo Birch from Texas explains that, several months after the Coronation, she was surprised when her mother proudly showed off a *Madame Alexander* Princess Elizabeth doll which had been packed away, wearing a new wig and a copy of the new Queen's coronation gown. Her mother showed her *The Life Magazine* pictures that she had used as a guide; Jo's mother was very creative, and, says Jo, it was lovely.

Coronation Composition

Although the 1950s was the era of the hard plastic doll, there were still plenty of composition dolls around, at least during the first half of the decade. (See Chapter 6). Gradually they ceased to sell, as children and their parents preferred the lightness and durability of plastic. Another form was more of a pottery-based mixture, and these are often called 'pot dolls'. Both kinds of composition were heavy and could crack or break when dropped.

Two companies which were famed for their speaking dolls at the time were *Peter Darling* and *Mark Payne*. These distinctive dolls were characterised by their over-long, very straight legs. In 1953, both companies produced large composition dolls which sang, amongst other things, 'God Save The Queen'. Each of these large, unwieldy dolls had a mechanism in her stomach operated by a protruding handle. When the handle was turned, it activated a disk which, rather scratchily, produced the sound of speech and song.

Interestingly, on the children's page in a 1953 issue of *Woman's Illustrated* magazine, a photo of the *Mark Payne* Royal Singing Doll was included. Also included was the following message from Pamela, (Chief Gnome!):

> She's wearing the Coronation Robes that follow the designs of the Queen's Dressmaker. When I was introduced her, she greeted me by singing 'God Save the Queen' and before I could get over my surprise – I'd never met a doll who could do that before – she started to recite poetry. That wasn't all. The Singing Doll can really laugh and cry, she walks and, even more exciting, her hair can be brushed and permed. If Mummy would like you to have a Singing Doll she can get details by writing to Harrow Sales, 256. Harrow Road, London, W.2

An In-Depth Look at a Mark Payne Composition Girl

Standing 26 inch high, this girl doll had a rather aloof air and was known as 'The Famous, Singing, Speaking and Walking Doll'. She has a rounded face with attractive colouring, sleep eyes, red lips and an open mouth with tiny teeth. Her short hair wig was made from mohair, and styled in a popular 'Marcel wave'. A metal handle protruded from her tummy, which, when turned, caused a shellac record to revolve, and a steel needle to play the recorded sound. The sound emanated through a paper diaphragm mounted on a small tin plate.

An instruction leaflet, together with a diagram, explained how to work the mechanism, and was headed:

Directions: Please read carefully and keep handy.

Push the little lever on left downwards until you hear a click, then release (do not keep

The voice mechanism of the Mark Payne doll was operated by turning a handle

your finger on the lever – the lever is always loose). This sets the mechanism to start.

Keep turning the handle fairly quickly, with a steady movement, the more evenly the better, you will soon find the best speed.

When you have reached the end of the 'singing' – push lever again as in direction 1, this resets the mechanism for starting again.

Do not turn the handle in the reverse direction, ie, Do not turn to the Left (that is anti-clockwise).

Special Note
This is a hand-worked mechanism. This handle must be turned continuously until the doll stops 'singing'.

How to make her walk:
Hold doll by her left arm and move her from foot to foot with a slight rocking movement from side to side.

This doll had an amazing repertoire; she said things such as 'Mummy, Mummy. Where have you been? Take me to London to see the Queen. What shall we see in London town? The Queen on her throne with her golden crown!' To finish up, she sang, of course, 'God Save Our Gracious Queen, Long live our noble Queen, God save the Queen'.

I am fortunate enough to own one of these talented dolls. She wears a long white satin gown, with a red cloak over the top, and has a royal blue sash to represent the order of the garter. Amazingly, her delicate cardboard crown has survived all these years, and it is studded with 'jewels'. Her white plastic shoes are of the Cinderella type and her undergarment is of particular interest; it is an all-in-one chemise with a specially made hole at the front to allow the handle of the singing mechanism to slot through.

These large dolls often come to light, and

Composition Queen doll
by Mark Payne

many of them are still preserved in their original boxes. Presumably, the dolls were rather large for everyday play and so their young owners tended to leave them alone. It's especially surprising when you come across the dolls which had been through the post. Many of the flimsy boxes bear postage stamps from around the time of the coronation, proving the dolls were sent by mail, and probably just tissue wrapped (there was no bubble wrap in those days!).

Also in 1953, an advertisement appeared in the *Daily Mirror* for a Coronation Doll, 'obtainable only from Peter Darling Ltd.', who operated from London's Grays Inn Road. With slogans such as "More than just a doll, she's a Darling Playmate" she was £4-15s-9d (£4.79) plus a post and packing charge of 4/- (20p). It wasn't necessary to pay all this as a lump sum (the average weekly wage at the time was only £5-2s-0d (£5.20)), she could be acquired for a 10/- (50p) deposit and 18 weekly payments of 5/- (25p). Apparently, callers were welcome, and both buses and trolley-buses passed near by.

The advertisement stated that she 'walks, sits, laughs, recites, sings and says her prayers in a real human voice.' Measuring 27 inches tall, she was a composition doll dressed in a long flouncy tiered gown, with a ribbon 'Order of the Garter' sash and a crown. She had 'combable hair and sleeping eyes' and was: 'A thrilling present and a wonderful coronation souvenir for your little girl.' This talented doll 'actually laughs he he he and says: I love my mummy. My mummy taught me a rhyme:

Composition Queen doll by Mark Payne

Little Bo Peep has lost her sheep
And doesn't know where to find them.
Leave them alone, and they'll come home
Bringing their tails behind them.

I CAN SING TOO!

Oh dear what can the matter be!
Oh dear what can the matter be!
Oh dear what can the matter be!
Johnny's so long at the fair.

Put me to bed mummy, 'cos I'm tired.
Now I lay me down to sleep,
I pray the Lord my soul to keep.
Goodnight, Mummy.'

If after all that, you weren't satisfied with the doll, there was a 'Money Refund Guarantee'.

The *Singing Doll Company*, owned by *Mark Payne Ltd*, in Harrow Road regularly advertised their large vociferous doll in the daily newspapers throughout the 1950s and 1960s. Though they were not of a particularly high quality, they had great novelty value and were relatively inexpensive. Additional records could be purchased

Roddy thumbs-up walker
dressed for the coronation

to increase their incredible repertoire, as well as a special shoulder bag in which the child could store these records. The records were sold in sets of three, having one song or rhyme on each side. A colourful range of outfits for the dolls was also available.

The Coronation was an excuse for manufacturers to dress dolls in velvet, silk and satin, and even today, well over 50 years since the event, the coronation theme is still popular. Manufacturers abroad sometimes dress their dolls in the coronation robes of the British Queen. *The Reliable Doll Company* (Canada) was just one of many who produced commemorative dolls in the 1950s, while *Madame Alexander* created a whole set of 36 dolls based on the Coronation. A beautiful Ginny appeared in 1984, complete with her crown, sceptre and a velvet, fur-trimmed robe. More recently the *Alexander* company issued a stunning, 2003, Jubilee Coronation Queen doll.

Celluloid soldiers from the 1950s

Chapter 3

Plastics and Pedigree

It's difficult now to imagine a world without plastic, but in the late 1940s, this new and exciting product revolutionised everyday living, creating a terrific stir in the toy industry. 'Plastic' (which actually means 'capable of being formed or moulded' and could really be applied to any modelling medium, such as clay) is a word we tend to use for a man-made malleable substance. It was not an alien substance as such, as plastic-type products had actually been around for some time. In 1862 an English chemist called Alexander Parkes had conducted a series of experiments, finally combining cellulose, various acids and castor oil to produce a material he called Parkesine. Parkesine was used for various small ornamental items. More familiar, perhaps, to us today is Bakelite, a form of plastic which often took on a mottled appearance. This was soon utilised in countless household, ornamental and industrial items.

Pedigree Delites

At one time there was a fashion for Bakelite jewellery, and many ladies of the 1930s and 1940s sported snakes-head bangles with jewelled eyes, in various colours of Bakelite. Another form of plastic was celluloid, a distinctive brittle substance which included camphor in the mixture. First invented in the 1870s, it proved particularly popular for toys and dolls. Even so, there were serious drawbacks to celluloid: not only was it prone to cracking and denting, it was a fire hazard. Many dreadful accidents had occurred when children left their toys on the hearth. Other plastic-type substances included Lucite and Xylonite. According to Kenneth D. Brown in his book *The British Toy Business*: 'With very few exceptions, no serious attempts had been made by toy firms to utilise plastics before the war, even though one expert had suggested there was likely to be a "most promising future" for "a carefully designed mouldable interlocking brick."

During the Second World War, most toy factories closed and the manufacturers switched to making munitions and industrial items. Often, they worked with a new, lightweight plastic material, cellulose acetate. Plastic was used for many applications during wartime, including cockpit instrument panels and electrical casings. After the hostilities ceased, and the factories reverted back to their original purpose, it was only natural that this wonderful, durable product was utilised in the making of toys and dolls. Plastics were released for toy manufacture in August 1945. The plastic dolls were made by a process known as injection moulding whereby molten plastic was forced into metal moulds and left till it set. Once hard and cooled, the two halves were glued or clipped together. Plastic was ideally suited to doll making, as it lent itself to more detailed casting, meaning that dolls could now have moulded hair, dimples and creases. Their faces no longer had to be smooth, as in the earlier porcelain and composition types. Soon, most of the major doll factories were producing plastic dolls.

Another plastics process, rotational casting, was developed in America in the early 1950s; the first application was a doll's head rotationally moulded in an oven using an electroformed nickel-copper mould and liquid PVC plastisol. This resulted in a moulding with no join line. In 1953, Eric Smith of *Rosebud Dolls* and John Orme, a toolmaker, heard of the new development and visited the US to see for themselves. They were so impressed that Eric commissioned John to make a similar oven, the first created for rotational moulding in Britain. One of the most famous doll companies of the 1950s era was *Pedigree Toys*, who were soon producing large quantities of plastic dolls.

Pedigree

Pedigree, a trade mark registered by *Lines Brothers Ltd* in 1942, is one of the most famous names in the British toy-making world, and over the years has been responsible for many of our best-loved dolls. Saucy Walker, Pretty Peepers, Delite, Elizabeth, Mandy-Lou, Beauty Skin, Sindy, Posey and First Love were all issued under the *Pedigree* name.

Lines Brothers was founded by three young men on their return from the First World War; William, Arthur and Walter Lines. Instead of joining the already established family business, which made baby carriages and wooden toys, the brothers decided to start afresh with a concern of their own.

At first, *G&L Lines Ltd.* concentrated on large items such as dolls houses, pedal cars and prams. In 1927 they registered the *Tri-ang* logo – a triangle, sometimes with 'Made in England' printed across, and sometimes containing a large 'L' inside the word 'Bros.' and with L. Bros., London, England along the three sides. The story goes that each of the three lines in the triangular trademark represented one of the Lines brothers. Right from the start, the emphasis was on quality toys, and the company soon gained an excellent reputation. Originally, *Lines Brothers* used premises in London, in the Old Kent Road, and by 1937 had acquired a new, large factory at Merton, also in London. Over the years the ambitious brothers obtained several factories both in Britain and abroad. They also owned showrooms and, at one time, even the majority of shares in Harrods.

In the late 1930s, they expanded into the doll world, and also produced a large range of stuffed toys. It was at this time that they published their first catalogue which used the *Pedigree* trade name, even though it wasn't officially registered till 1942. This 1937 catalogue featured an array of soft toys and dolls, and is a veritable delight for any doll collector. The range was stunning especially when compared to modern doll manufacturers, who might only issue a few dolls at any one time. This catalogue included five different sizes of all-composition dolls, ranging from 10 inches to 20 inches, with a choice of painted eyes or the metal sleeping kind. Black skinned versions were sold too. In all, nearly 50 different types and sizes of baby dolls were featured, in a variety of styles, either all composition, or composition-headed on a soft body.

The composition used for these early *Pedigree* dolls must have been a substantial mix, because so many of the dolls are still around in good condition. Made from woodflour, these dolls were advertised as being 'almost unbreakable'. Probably, the easiest to find today of these early dolls are small bent-limbed babies with painted side-glance eyes. These delightful dolls, around 10 inches tall, were the perfect size for a young child to hold. Although they must have been regularly dropped and generally handled quite roughly, most are still quite presentable, apart from showing a few scuffs or a little slight crazing. These baby dolls were sold either ready dressed wearing a dress and bonnet (or a romper suit) or were sold unclothed except for a nappy. At the time, baby dolls were amazingly popular, as demonstrated by this catalogue.

Straight-legged composition girl and

Composition baby by Lines Brothers (Pedigree) 1930s

boy dolls were also sold, some in regional costumes, others wearing romper suits or dresses, while a range of 17 inch Streamline Dolls had slimmer bodies and legs. A catalogue supplement dated 1939/40 boasted: 'British made throughout in our new Hygienic Doll Factory. All *Pedigree* dolls have jointed arms and legs. The dresses are by expert designers, and only the best material is used.'

When the war broke out, as the factory was classified as a maker of 'luxury goods', it was switched to war work, and was soon involved in the manufacture of munitions and guns. This change must have been a shock to the workers, used to seeing gentle dolls and soft toys roll off the production line.

According to Colette Mansell, as the brothers had seen action in the Great War, they decided no war-like toys would ever be made in their factories. The three men must have been devastated when their premises were used to produce Sten guns, shell cases and experimental rocket-propelled aircraft.

After the war, *Pedigree* soon began to create dolls using plastic, from the tiniest of babies to life-sized toddlers. In a relatively short period of around 12 years, from 1945 to the late 1950s, *Lines Brothers*, under their *Pedigree* name, designed and produced a huge range of hard plastic dolls. Many of these dolls are now regarded as classics, and they are becoming extremely collectable, especially innovative dolls such as Beauty Skin, Saucy Walker and Pretty Peepers.

An In-Depth Look at a Pedigree Pretty Peepers

Pretty Peepers was introduced by *Pedigree* in 1957. This pretty doll utilised the face of an earlier doll, the 1953 Saucy Walker. Made from hard plastic, she stood 22 inches tall and featured short curly saran hair. She had an open mouth with a tongue and two top teeth, and her back was marked 'Pedigree, Made in England'. Pretty Peepers was a knee-joint doll, and these special joints meant that she could sit properly in a chair or even kneel. If her hand was held, and she was guided, she could walk and her head moved from side to side. At first glance this doll resembled the knee-jointed dolls which had been issued by *Pedigree* two years earlier – however, there was one major difference. It is this difference that makes her so collectable and difficult to find today.

Inside Pretty Peeper's chest was a special mechanism, which was disguised on the outside as an oblong plate, measuring 2 inches by 1 inch. The mechanism was operated by the plate which, when depressed, connected to a device inside the doll's head. This caused the position of the eyes to move – and it even changed their colour. Years later, the *Palitoy* Company was to issue a 'revolutionary' teen doll with a large head containing colour-change eyes – but in reality, *Pedigree* had already beaten them to it, by 25 years! So, in a way, Pretty Peepers was a forerunner of the 1970s Blythe doll.

Pedigree Pretty Peepers showing brown eyes

Pedigree Pretty Peepers showing blue eyes

Pretty Peepers could look forward or glance to the right or left and her eyes could also turn from blue to brown. Although they could close, it was also possible to make the eyes stay open even when the doll was lying on her back in her pram. If the chest plate was activated while the doll was on her back, her eyes closed, they remained open if the chest plate was pressed while she was sitting up.

The eye sequence of the Pretty Peepers doll was as follows:

Brown eyes front
Brown eyes left glance
Brown eyes right glance
Blue eyes front
Blue eyes right glance
Blue eyes left glance

Her clothing was distinctive, and included an ingenious all-in-one romper-like garment which consisted of a white cotton blouse with puffed sleeves and peter pan collar. The leg openings were trimmed with woollen braid. This garment allowed the chest plate to be operated without undressing the doll and fastened with two poppers at the back. Over the top, Pretty Peepers wore a colourful, red or yellow, felt pinafore with a heart-shaped bib-top, edged with woollen braid. Ribbons secured the bib-top in place, and the pinafore was fastened at the side with one popper. It bore a 'Pedigree Made in England' silk label. The outfit was completed with white socks and shoes.

The earlier Saucy Walker was a 22 inch hand-assisted walker with flirting eyes, which gave her a cheeky expression. Saucy Walker was introduced by *Pedigree* about five years before Pretty Peepers, and is much easier to find today. She is a great favourite with doll collectors, a well made substantial doll with attractive blushing to face, knees and hands. Saucy Walker turned her head from side to side as she walked

Pedigree Saucy Walker

and could 'cry' as she had a mama unit fitted into her back. Her mohair wig came in various col-ours and styles, and her open mouth revealed two top teeth. Facially she was identical both to Pretty Peepers and to the Knee-Bend or Knee-Joint. Knee-Jointed dolls became very popular in the mid-1950s, and were produced by several other companies including *Roddy* and *Rosebud*. The Knee-Joint catalogue entry says, 'This is the newest type of doll for 1955 and Pedigree are the creators as usual,' adding: 'This lovely young lady possesses all the qualities which have made Pedigree walking dolls world famous and, most important of all, her knees are fully jointed so that natural sitting, lying and kneeling positions are possible'. Apparently, these dolls were intended to kneel alongside their little owners for bedtime prayers, conjuring up a touching picture. *Pedigree* also stated that: 'her hair is the finest Saran which may be brushed, combed and shampooed'.

Pedigree were justly proud of their range of large, 22 inch hard plastic walking dolls, and the leaflet which accompanied them stated:

> *This fine precision moulded walking doll is a perfect example of British craftsmanship at its best. Like all Pedigree dolls, it has been created by a RA exhibiting sculptor who specialises in true-to-life doll design and is exquisitely dressed in beautifully fashioned clothes.*

The walking doll is robustly constructed of non-inflammable material and is virtually unbreakable. The eyes have sleeping and flirting movements and a talking voice is also incorporated. Treated carefully, this doll will give a lifetime's pleasure. It should not be immersed in water nor exposed to excessive heat.

The following simple instructions should be observed:-

1. The Pedigree walking doll stands quite erect on its own two feet.
2. To make the doll sit down hold it firmly move the legs <u>one at a time</u> – forward at right angles to the body. <u>It is most important that only one leg be moved at a time</u>.
3. Walking: - See that the doll is standing in an upright position with both arms at its side. Move the arm nearest you upwards and forwards until you feel that it is fully extended so that the doll is standing with one arm outstretched. Hold the doll firmly by the hand and wrist, and lead it forward by putting the weight of the doll on the leg which is not moving, so as to enable the other leg to take one pace forward. Keep the doll upright all the time, rocking it slightly from side to side during walking.
4. Always treat your Pedigree walking doll carefully – although it is very strongly made and will stand up to a great deal of rough treatment, a little care will be worthwhile.

It then cautions:

As you know, when you have been playing you sometimes get grubby, and Mummy has to wash your hands and legs, so if your doll's hand's and legs also get grubby you must do as Mummy does and wash them with a soft flannel, soap and warm water. You must NOT use hot water and must take great care not to let any water get near the eyes or the Mama voice or inside the doll, for if you do, you will cause it considerable harm.

Pedigree knee-joint girl

Important
This doll is fitted with a detachable Mama Voice, which you can replace in
the event of failure. You should be able to obtain a replacement from your
local stockist, but if any difficulty write direct to us.

The address given was: *International Model Aircraft Ltd.*, Morden Road, Merton, London, SW19. This had been a subsidiary of *Lines Brothers*, owners of *Pedigree Dolls*, since 1932. Walter Lines later stated that he had acquired an interest in 'the first flying model aeroplane which ever looked remotely like the real thing.' Two years later, Lines had a new production facility built at Merton. An important benefit gained from *International Model Aircraft* was a facility for plastic injection moulding, and by 1935 this process was being utilised for *Tri-ang* toys including clockwork vehicles. Like many other factories of the time, cessation of producing toys during the war meant that major advances in doll manufacture ceased until the mid to late forties, although on-going research was still possible due to the plastics used in wartime construction.

Lines Brothers continued to expand, and amongst their other acquisitions was the *Rovex* factory, which they wanted because they were interested in the slot car racing toy, Scalextric. Perhaps, though, their most famous doll premises, apart from those in Morden Road, was the factory which the company moved to in Canterbury in the early 1960s. The Canterbury factory was to become famed as the birthplace of many beautiful vinyl dolls in the 1960s.

Author's childhood Pedigree Delite girl, known as 'Janice'

Pedigree character Dutch girl

Another popular series of *Pedigree* dolls were the so-called Delite dolls, which encompassed a whole range from tiny babies to larger toddlers. All are charming and many featured exceptionally sweet faces, proving very popular with today's collectors. The smallest straight-legged kind were often dressed in regional or fancy costumes. Bent-limbed baby Delites are amongst the easiest of the *Pedigree* hard plastic dolls to find, they were exceedingly well loved when they were first made and most collectors have at least one of these delightful dolls. Many of the Delites could also be bought undressed, ready for the child or her mother to knit or sew for at home.

Pedigree, whose boxes and catalogues were a mine of information, stated on the box of a small Delite girl, 'A sculptor designed baby doll fully jointed with straight legs and moving eyes with lashes. Precision moulding for true to life definition of limbs.'

The 7 inch Character dolls were popular. First introduced in the late 1940s, these cuties with moulded or wigged hair and open, 'starfish' hands came dressed in a huge variety of costumes. Amongst them were Jack Tar, Fairy, Highland Laddie, Tommy Atkins, PC49, Sloppy Joe, Buffalo Bill and Swiss Girl. In 1950, these little dolls were supplied to retailers at various prices, starting at around 38/- (£1.90) per dozen. Interestingly, three years later, the price had been reduced slightly to 36/- (£1.80). Sadly, the arms on these dolls seem very prone to hard plastic disease and many are found with arms which have turned white or have blistered (see Chapter 10).

A distinctive *Pedigree* toddler was issued in the early 1950s – the clockwork walker. Obtainable as either a boy or girl (girls wore a wig, boys had moulded hair), these dolls were operated by a large metal key. There were two sizes, 14 inch and $8^1/2$ inches. The small size had a character-type face. In 1955, several other $8^1/2$ inch dolls were added to the range. These included Jock a Scotsman, Jazzy an orchestral conductor, Steve a jockey, Monty, a top-hatted gentleman and Joey, a clown. The catalogue stated: 'A few turns of the key on the powerful clockwork mechanism and away these amazing dolls toddle over long distances. Attractively dressed'.

An In-Depth Look at a Pedigree Clockwork Walker

Standing 14 inches high, this sturdy doll has an enchanting face with a pointed chin, similar to that found in the Baby Delite range. He is completely made from hard plastic, with the clockwork key mechanism protruding from his back. This Clockwork Walker's head has moulded curls, so we can assume he is intended as a boy, though, as he wears pink, he can be of either gender. He has rounded cheeks, blue sleep eyes, an open-closed mouth revealing two tiny teeth and a moulded tongue. His back is marked, 'Pedigree made in England. Patent applied for.'

Clockwork Walker dolls feature moulded socks and shoes – the shoes are quite substantial to aid walking, however the dolls still tend to wobble and fall, invariably cracking, which is presumably why they are difficult to find today. This example is wearing his original cotton romper suit trimmed with a Peter Pan collar, and which fastens with two poppers at the back. The romper has a fabric *Pedigree* label sewn into the back seam. The large

Pedigree clockwork toddler walker

metal key, which bears the *Tri-ang* logo, fits into a hole in the doll's back. As this is wound a satisfactory whirring noise can be heard, an evocative sound which instantly brings memories of clockwork trains, cars and other toys from earlier years. (A time before everything was battery-operated!) This doll would never pass today's strict safety laws, as he has large coiled metal springs which protrude from each leg socket – which must have been a finger hazard – but he is a lovely doll and would have been fun for a child. When he was new, he was priced at 15/8d (74p).

Pedigree clockwork toddler walker showing key mechanism

Amongst the other dolls made by *Pedigree* in the 1950s were the Pin-Up fashion series – similar to Elizabeth (see Chapter 2) – dolls with attractive rounded faces and rosy cheeks, though not as curvy and voluptuous as later teens were to become. There was a choice of two sizes, 14 inches and 19 inches, and the dolls had names such as Hazel, Enid and Alice. Another doll in the series was Nurse Nan, who, as her name suggests, was attired in a nurse's outfit of striped dress, white apron, head-dress and cape. Pin-Ups came with *Revlon*'s Pin Up play perm which included sets of hair curlers.

Pedigree Pin-Up advertisement 1950s

Pedigree black toddler and baby

Consequently many of the dolls found today tend to have matted wigs where budding young hairdressers had practised their skills. Pin-Up dolls were advertised in *Picture Post* in 1952 as having 'magic nylon hair'. The advert went on to say:

We're darlings of dolls and we're looking for mothers just like you. Our big blue eyes open and close, and we wear the prettiest clothes…all so different and gay. And oh! Our lovely long nylon hair! Some of us are glamorous blondes and some the prettiest brunettes. See us all at your toyshop and choose who you want most! And just imagine! You can perm our lovely hair over and over and over again. Perm it in all sorts of different styles with a Pin-Up perm kit of your very own! Hurry along to your toyshop and see these wonderful new Pin-Up dolls for yourself! Make sure it's the very next present you get! (A Pin-Up doll with a Pin-Up Play Perm costs exactly 59/6 complete). A Pin-Up Play Perm Kit comes with every Pin-Up doll… (Kit includes Pin-Up Play perm Lotion, Crème Shampoo, 10 curlers and tissues, comb and illustrated instruction booklet). Important Pin-Up Play perm Lotion Guaranteed SAFE.

How's that for pester-power?!

Some of the biggest dolls were the Brighton Belles. Large enough to wear a toddler's clothes, they stood 28 inches tall, and were difficult to carry, being straight-legged. These were the kind of dolls, which, after being admired, tended to be left alone as they didn't fit into a pram or pushchair.

Pedigree produced various other walking dolls, including the black Mandy Lou, a 20 inch girl with exaggerated bright red lips. Made from shiny black plastic she featured a short astrakhan wig and could walk if a child held her hands. Her sibling, Dixie, was the same height. The company also made a black open/closed mouth walker with similar curly astrakhan hair, in a range of sizes, as well as a 'dusky' walker (light chocolate coloured) doll with longer black hair styled into two plaits.

Pedigree 'dusky' walker

Chapter 4

Other Major Companies

The majority of the doll factories in the United Kingdom soon switched across to the plastics, realising that children – and their parents – always wanted to be in with the latest craze (just as today). Plastic dolls had so much going for them that children scorned the 'old fashioned' composition types, and if a company wanted to prosper, they had to keep up with the times.

A large proportion of hard plastic dolls were, rather grandly, referred to as 'walkie-talkies' – they could 'walk' if a child held their arm or waist to guide them, and they could say mama. The mama voice was achieved by a bellows-operated cylindrical metal or plastic box fitted into the doll's back, with just the grille on view. When tilted, it caused a wail, which, with a bit of imagination, could be thought to sound like 'mama'. Some manufacturers, with a bit more honesty, called them crying dolls.

Palitoy

One of the greatest names in the world of toys, this company gave us some of our most classic dolls, though mainly 1960s and 1970s vinyl, a little later than the scope of this book.

The company, originally known as *Cascelloid*, was founded in 1919 by Arthur Pallett, at first concentrating on celluloid household items. It later progressed to small toys before making its first dolls in the mid-1920s, and having great success with a range of celluloid Mabel Lucie Attwell dolls, including the character Diddums who featured in many of her paintings. There was also a range of celluloid girls (called Anne), boys (Tony), and babies (Dinky Babies). Although the company adopted the *Palitoy* trademark in 1932, they were still using the *Cascelloid* name into the mid-1960s. When *Cascelloid* became an subsidiary of *British Xylonite*, in 1937, it acquired a factory at Coalville, Leicestershire, and there they developed a new product called Plastex, which was a composition mix. They used this product for a range of dolls which they advertised as 'virtually unbreakable,' and still easily found today is a bent-limbed bald baby called Priscilla, a tribute to Plastex and its durability.

Cascelloid/Palitoy was requisitioned during the war for the manufacture of munitions, and when hostilities ceased, switched to the new 'wonder product' of injection-moulded cellulose acetate. This product had been developed through the war and nowadays we refer to it as 'hard plastic'. Along with the other British doll makers, *Palitoy* discovered that this new product revitalised the doll industry, and was soon producing classic dolls, such as the 'Girl' doll - a tie-in with the highly-popular *Girl* comic, Belinda (a doll with a marching action), Petal Skin dolls and the Patsy hard rubber type (see Chapter 6). The company also made extra large size, 30 inch, hard plastic dolls, capable of wearing the clothes of a small child. They were advertised as having sleep eyes and 'plastic filament hair'.

An In-Depth Look at a Palitoy 'Girl' Doll

The Girl doll was issued as a tie-in to the very popular *Girl* comic, which had been launched in 1951 by Hulton Press, as a companion to the *Eagle* comic for boys. It was advertised as being published 'Every Wednesday Price 4^1/2 d' (2p). *Girl* was a quality comic, printed on glossy paper and with plenty of colour. Adventures in strip-story

The 'Girl' doll was issued by Palitoy in conjunction with Girl comic

The 'Girl' doll, Palitoy

The 'Girl' logo on the 'Girl' doll's belt, Palitoy

format told of characters such as Nurse Susan of St. Bride's, Wendy and Jinx, Belle of the Ballet, and Lettice Leefe 'The Greenest Girl in School'. As with similar children's publications of the time, the comic had its own club with a badge. The Girl badge was unusual; rather than the usual round metal badge, this was a bronze-coloured profile of a girl's head, and this logo also appeared on the comic's header. So it was only to be expected that when the *Girl* comic launched its own doll, she was well decorated with *Girl* logos.

The Girl doll was produced by *Palitoy* (Cascelloid) in 1953, a 14 inch tall walker whose head turned from side to side as she moved. She was jointed at neck, hips and shoulders. Her legs were straight, her arms slightly curved, and her dainty hands had long, delicate fingers. Pretty, in the slightly old-fashioned style of the Pin-Up dolls, she was made from shiny plastic and her solemn face featured delicate colouring and the famous *Palitoy* lavender-coloured eyes. Originally her hair was tightly curled around the edges, though as children enjoyed combing and brushing the hair, dolls found today often lack most of the curls. *Palitoy* encouraged this, claiming 'Her hair can be washed, combed and curled.' They explained that you needed to wet the hair with warm water and rub in shampoo 'until you have a good lather.' Afterwards it was necessary to rinse, towel dry, comb and wind the hair onto curlers, before combing into the desired style.

Girl wore a short white taffeta dress which was printed with red *Girl* logos, and trimmed with red ric-rac braid around the neck, hem and sleeves. Underneath, she wore matching knickers. Her red ribbon belt fastened with a white plastic buckle, fashioned in the shape of the *Girl* logo, and the dress secured at the back with two small silver poppers. Even her hair ribbon was printed with the *Girl* logo, in either blue or red. She had white socks and red or white shoes. The *Girl* doll was marked 'Palitoy Made in England' on her back, with the wording arranged in a circle and the number 35 in the centre.

Palitoy claimed that the dress could be washed: 'Tub it gently in warm, soapy water and remember – never twist the fabric.' Today's collectors, however, usually avoid attempting to wash the dresses, fearing that the red colour will run. Extra patterns for the Girl doll were advertised in the *Girl* comic, and they cost 10d, (4p), including postage and packing! The patterns included an overcoat; blouse and skirt; cape and skirt; bloomer suit; sun dress and stole; square dancing outfit; nightie and a long, full-skirted party dress.

Instructions to make Girl walk read: 'Move the arm you want to hold slowly upwards till you hear it click, then lead your doll forwards. She will walk with you easily, especially if you let her rock slightly from side to side. If you push her down gently her legs will click into a sitting position. Raise her, and her legs will fall back into the position ready for walking.' The instructions added reassuringly: 'She is practically unbreakable but, if you do break off her arms and legs, you will be able to obtain new limb parts from the makers, Palitoy.'

A particularly popular line of *Palitoy* dolls were the tiny, 4 inch, bent limbed babies, which were sold quite cheaply in shops such as Woolworths. (See Chapter 1.) These babies often came in little raffia or wicker cribs and were probably intended for dolls houses, though many children invested their pocket money into buying several, which they used to play schools or hospitals. Clearly marked, they have a distinctive shiny appearance and hands with a pointing left finger. Other dolls included the Pin-Up range of dolls and the Marchers, a type of plastic dolls who swung their arms with a vigorous marching action as they walked. However, it was the 1960s/1970s which were the golden years for *Palitoy* so far as design and innovation were concerned.

An In-Depth Look at a Palitoy Marcher

This Marcher dates from 1952 and is a hard plastic doll with an odd marching action, swinging her arms as she walks. She stands 20 inches high and is marked on her back, 'Palitoy Made in England. Prov. Pat 13313/50'. She is also marked on the back of her neck, 'Made in England' together with 'PAT 535811 Foreign Patents'. The *Palitoy* Marcher doll has flirty eyes, an open mouth with two top teeth

Palitoy 'Marcher' doll

and a tongue and a soft mohair wig. Her legs seem rather short for her body, giving her a rather stumpy appearance, and her tummy is rather plump, almost bulgy, with a seventeen hole grid indicating the presence of a mama unit. Her hands and feet are very well moulded, the fingers are delicately splayed and the toes long and shapely. Two screws at the top of her back and a further two just below hip level allow access to the body mechanism if needed. (See Chapter 7 for Transitional Model).

Roddy

Just like so many other British toy companies, the *Roddy* company underwent a chequered history, experiencing several mergers. Its founder, Daniel George Todd, was a managing director at a Lancashire company called *Toy Time Toys*. Amongst the products it made were composition and soft-bodied dolls; in the late 1940s, Daniel decided to form a company which would concentrate on doll production, especially using the new plastics, but would also produce composition dolls, many of which Daniel designed. This company was called *D.G. Todd*, but unless you can find a boxed example, its products are difficult to identify as many of the dolls were unmarked. It then began using the trade name *Rodnoid*, and this name is sometimes found stamped on the back of small hard plastic baby dolls.

Rodnoid dolls are not particularly easy to find as they were made for such as short time, but amongst them were small, 3 inch tall, bald baby dolls with fixed painted eyes, jointed at shoulders and hips, which were often used in dolls houses. Some of the larger *Rodnoid* dolls had sleep eyes and, occasionally, mohair wigs. Often these dolls were sold through *J. Cowan Dolls Ltd*, sole distributors for *D. G. Todd* in Britain. Very soon it was discovered that the *Rodnoid* name was similar to that of another manufacturer so the trade name *Roddy* was registered instead, formed from a combination of Robinson and Todd. (Robinson was a partner in the firm.)

Roddy and Rodnoid babies

Small Roddy
and box

SLEEPING EYES

Roddy pouting
face baby

Roddy thumbs-up
baby with tin eyes

Early *Roddy* hard plastic dolls had eyes made from tin. The white, iris and pupil are transfer-printed on. Frequently, later ones had plastic eyes with integral solid plastic lashes. These lashes were moulded onto the eyeball, though the company did make many other dolls with conventional hair lashes. *Roddy* dolls seem quite popular with today's collectors, especially the little hard plastic 'thumbs-up' *Roddy* dolls, characterised by their clenched fists and raised thumbs. This peculiarity, though, was shared by a few other manufacturers, who also favoured the clenched hand moulding. Many of these early *Roddy* dolls are made from an extra glossy plastic, which is very attractive. In the 1950s, the smaller sizes were particularly popular with schoolgirls, as they were an ideal size to sew or knit for, and could easily be tucked away into a blazer pocket or school satchel. These 6 inch tall dolls with their sweet smiles and chubby cheeks are enchanting.

Roddy smiling face girl

Additionally *Roddy* produced a 9 inch tall thumbs-up, with a yes/no feature – when the button on her front was pressed, she nodded yes, while the button on her back made her shake her head. Larger thumbs-up dolls were hand-assisted walkers, with various expressions, whose heads turned as they moved. These were available in both white and chocolate. Often, the smaller sizes of hard plastic *Roddy* dolls have moulded or painted shoes. If you find one with silver shoes, then she was probably intended as a fairy. Many small *Roddy* dolls were purchased undressed by other companies or individuals and redressed in costumes to appeal to collectors; Welsh and Scottish being particularly common.

There were three favourite *Roddy* faces, one with puffed cheeks and a pout, one with an open-mouthed smile, and the third with a delightfully-solemn face. This latter face must have proved particularly popular, as when the company changed over to using vinyl in the mid 1950s, she was issued in the new medium. In addition they made a range of serious-faced Knee-bend girl dolls which could easily sit on a chair or kneel, thanks to the special joint in their legs. Knee-bend dolls were also made by *Pedigree* and *Rosebud*, and were a popular line at the time.

Roddy serious face girl

An In-Depth Look at a Roddy Thumbs-Up Walker

This *Roddy* Thumbs-up Walker is dressed as a boy, though can look equally good as a girl. However, a wigged girl version was also available. He is made from an attractive high gloss plastic, which is seen in many *Roddy* dolls, and this one dates from the early 1950s. A fraction under 12 inches tall, he has the pout face with puffed cheeks, looking for all the world as though he is about to whistle. His face colouring is perfect, he is as mint as when left the *Roddy* factory over 55 years ago, and he features sleep eyes, hair lashes and red closed lips. The hair has been coloured a rich brown, and his cheeks are flushed pink. His clenched fists are moulded into a 'thumbs up' position, the right fist also having one pointing finger, while his feet have moulded strap shoes and his back is marked 'Roddy Made in England'.

Roddy thumbs-up pouty boy walker

During the 1950s *D. G. Todd* registered several doll names including Walking Princess which was used on a range of teen-type dolls. Also registered were Babs, Fifi, Julie, Bubble, Joan and Edna. The most unusual doll, and certainly the most difficult to find today, is Edna, who dates from 1955. Edna, 18 inches, was a slim young lady whose joints resemble those found in dolls of a much earlier era. Even though made from hard plastic, Edna's body somehow resembled that of a bisque doll. It was jointed at the neck, waist, shoulders, hips, knees and elbows. This doll featured the favourite solemn *Roddy* face and was really beautiful. The majority

Roddy walking doll with moulded plastic dress

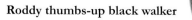

Roddy thumbs-up black walker

of hard plastic *Roddy* dolls are clearly marked on their backs and necks 'Made in England' and with the word *Roddy* which is underlined. Those supplied to other companies were not always marked, but were sometimes encased in polythene bags bearing header cards.

A particularly quaint *Roddy* novelty was a small walking doll dating from around 1950, just 6 inches high. Her plastic dress was moulded onto her body, and came in several colours including pink, blue and green. Amongst other *Roddy* favourites are the gorgeous Topsy type black babies with three woolly tufts of 'hair' on their heads, the so-called 'Floating head' 12 inch walkers which feature an odd walking method – a rod connects the head with the crutch, causing the head to swing – and the tiny, 3 inch dolls often used in dolls houses.

An In-Depth Look at a Roddy Black Thumbs-Up (Topsy) Baby

This delightful black baby, with a distinctive top-knot of hair, is nowadays often to referred to as a Topsy baby by collectors. She is $8^1/2$ inches high, and features a typical bent-leg baby body. Her sleep eyes are amber, and do not have lashes, her lips are red, her head is fixed to the body, moulded all in one, and she is jointed at shoulders and hips with brown elastic. The 'hair', actually black mohair, is arranged in three tufts on top of her head, the rest of the head being bald but with strands of moulded hair at the nape. Her pierced ears hold metal hoop earrings. She is marked 'Roddy Made in England' across her back. Her hands are modelled in clenched fists with the thumbs pointing upwards and the forefinger of the right hand is also pointing.

Dolls in this style earned the

Roddy black 'Topsy' baby

nickname Topsy in reference to the little girl character in *Uncle Tom's Cabin* by Harriet Beecher Stowe. The three-tufts-of-hair style has cropped up regularly over the years, especially in 1920s/1930s black composition dolls. These dolls were often sold wearing just a few strings of beads and a simple cotton or raffia skirt.

Roddy made the transition to the softer plastics quite easily in the mid-1950s (see Chapter 7) and continued making dolls until the mid-1960s when they were acquired by Scottish buyers, Alex and James Smith. The new owners decided to alter the *Roddy* trade name to *Bluebell*.

Rosebud

Perhaps it was the face, perhaps it was the clothing, perhaps it was the style – or maybe it was just the pretty name – but by the 1950s, every little girl wanted a *Rosebud* doll. Even today, *Rosebud*s are top of many collectors' lists, with Miss Rosebud being very much sought after.

The company didn't always have such a pretty name. Originally it was known as *Nene Plastics*, and was started by Eric Smith in the 1940s. Earlier, in 1934, Smith had taken over a family business which specialised in the manufacture of wooden toys, and soon decided to branch out into the doll world. At first he experimented with a composition-type mix before following the modern trend and switching to plastics.

There is an often-quoted story that in 1947 a little girl was visiting the factory and she admired the dolls, comparing their lips to rosebuds. Whether

Rosebud thumbsuck baby

true or not, it is a delightful thought, and maybe one day that little girl will come forward. What we do know, however, is that the trademark *Rosebud* was registered in that year, and soon thousands of beautiful hard plastic dolls were pouring forth from the Northamptonshire *Rosebud* factories, originally at Raunds, later at Wellingborough. Eventually, they were turning out 10,000,000 dolls a year and exporting them to 72 countries.

Rosebud's earliest plastic dolls were a range of 7 inch girl and boy dolls and 6 inch babies. The babies soon became affectionately known as Thumbsucks or Suckathumbs on account of their bent right arms with a sticking-up thumb, perfect for sucking! Sometimes the babies were bald, and, more rarely, they were given mohair wigs. They had sweet expressions and sleep eyes which were either painted or made of glassene. These charming babies were jointed at shoulders and hips, and their legs were bent.

The popular small girl and boy dolls, which came in both white and black versions, had fixed heads and unjointed straight legs. Their arms were jointed at the shoulders. They tended to have a kind of 'sucked lemon' look, and their eyes were painted (early) or glassene (later 1950s). They were produced in the 1960s too, but the faces were changed slightly and they had larger eyes. Girl dolls wore mohair wigs in various shades, and the boy dolls had moulded hair. This moulded hair could also be seen underneath the girls' wigs; it saved manufacturing costs to be able to get both head types using one mould, and this popular device

Rosebud girl and box, all ready for dressing

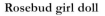
Rosebud girl doll

of moulded hair under a wig was often seen in the 1950s. It also meant that if the hair came off – something which often happened with mohair wigs – the doll was still fairly presentable underneath.

The catalogue description read, 'The popular Rosebud Miniatures include 6 inch babies dressed or undressed and attractive 7 inch models, undressed or in a variety of costumes. There are fairies, brides, sailors and many others. All are in lightweight plastic and have sleeping eyes.'

The undressed versions were popular as models for the knitting patterns which appeared in magazines of the time, especially *Woman's Weekly* which featured the Twins regularly. Dozens of pretty outfits were created for them. (See Chapter 8.)

An In-Depth Look at a Rosebud Miss Rosebud

Today's collectors adore Miss Rosebud. This very pretty girl stands almost 8 inches tall and has sleeping eyes, a mohair wig, a slightly chubby face and an endearing superior expression. She is jointed at neck, shoulders and hips, and is marked 'Miss Rosebud' on her back. Miss Rosebud dates from the early 1950s and at the time cost 3/11d. (19p) but today is worth much more. The catalogue stated: 'Each young lady in the Rosebud family has a personality of her own and is dressed accordingly – a model of careful grooming with a stylish coiffure and an ensemble correct in

Miss Rosebud

Miss Rosebud

every detail.' Miss Rosebud was still being produced in the early 1960s, but some of the moulds had been sold to other companies including *Amanda Jane* who turned her into Jinx.

Naturally, *Rosebud* made larger dolls too, most of them featuring the rounded face which was so distinctive of *Rosebud* hard plastic dolls. A particularly pretty range were the 13 inch, 15 inch and 17 inch hard plastic girl dolls of the mid-1950s. Sweet-faced, with rather solemn expressions, these resembled sturdy toddlers and had sleep eyes, rosy cheeks, and mohair wigs, which came in a variety of styles and colours. *Rosebud* also sold some of the dolls naked, ready to dress at home.

There were also knee-bend girls with a joint in the knee, which enabled them to sit properly in a chair without their legs sticking out straight. As we have seen, several companies were producing knee-jointed dolls at the time, but the joints often broke with rough or heavy play. Knee-jointed dolls are worth seeking out; they always look good in a doll collection as they pose so well.

An In-Depth Look at a Rosebud Knee-bend/ Knee-joint

This Knee-Jointed doll, by *Rosebud*, is 17 inches high. She has a rounded, almost chubby face, sleep eyes and a closed mouth with a slight smile. Her lashes are plastic, she has delicate, fine eyebrows and her face paint is excellent with a gentle blush on her cheeks. This *Rosebud*'s wig is made from brown mohair, but she was available in several hair shades.

She is a walking doll, and is jointed at neck, shoulders, hips and knees. When she is required to sit, the knees must be gently bent to lock the joint. This knee-jointed doll is marked 'Made in England' across her back, but

Rosebud knee-joint girl

her distinctive, gentle smile leaves no doubt that she was made by the *Rosebud* company. A smaller version, 13 inches, was also available, as well as a black doll. Later, she reappeared with a vinyl head, featuring rooted hair. (See Chapter 7.)

Rosebud featured an extensive range of baby dolls in various sizes, some with open-closed mouths and two top teeth, while others had no teeth or closed mouths. Baby dolls came in white or black versions, and a catalogue of the time shows a pretty baby girl in dress and bonnet together with an undressed baby. The caption states, 'Prettily dressed dolls like this, and chubby lifelike dolls like the one below, are typical of the Rosebud babies. Beautifully modelled in strong, matt-finished lightweight plastic, they are fully jointed and have sleeping eyes. From 6 inch to 17 inch (with mama voice from $11^1/2$ inch and upwards).'

By the mid to late 1950s, *Rosebud* were experimenting with vinyl, a material more pliable and which could be moulded to show more detail than hard plastic. (See Chapter 7.) Sadly, in 1967, *Rosebud* was acquired by *Mattel*, and after a while the pretty name disappeared. There was a glimmer of hope that the name might reappear when, in the 1970s, the Wellingborough factory became *Rotary Plastics*, and applied to use the *Rosebud* name, as *Mattel* no longer seemed to need it. As permission was refused they became *Blossom Toys*, producing a large range of vinyl dolls.

Rosebud girl

Chapter 5

Smaller Companies

Amanda Jane

When the *Amanda Jane* company was founded in 1952 by Conrad and Elsin Rawnsley it initially specialised in the making and supplying of top-quality dolls' shoes and clothes, a venture which proved highly successful. Thousands of garments were produced, to suit dolls of a large range of sizes, and jewellery, belts, slippers, handbags and umbrellas were also supplied – all the accessories a doll could possibly want or need. At first, the company was based in the Rawnsley's London home, but eventually, in the late 1950s, they moved to Halfway Mill, Petworth, Sussex. Then it was decided to produce a small doll, together with a range of clothes to fit her. They called the doll Jinx, and today she is a favourite amongst collectors of small hard plastic dolls.

An In-Depth Look at an Amanda Jane Jinx

Jinx was very similar to other small hard plastic dolls of the day, notably Miss Rosebud, *Faerie Glen*'s Tonie and Sally, small *Roddy* dolls and the American Ginny. She was cast in hard shiny plastic from an old *Rosebud* mould, using the injection moulding method, by *Wilkinson and Gross* of London, and was made up of 12 parts glued together – jointed at neck, shoulders and hips by elastic bands. Jinx,

Jinx by Amanda Jane

who first appeared in 1958, was 8 inches tall, and across her back was the word 'England'. There was no company name on the doll; this didn't appear until *Amanda Jane* began making their vinyl ranges in the early 1960s. Just like Miss Rosebud, Jinx was a little girl type, not a teen, and was quite chubby with small sleep eyes and a solemn expression. Her hair was a short mohair wig (though occasionally plaited versions appear).

According to an early Jinx booklet, 8 inch Jinx came wearing a choice of wigs. The Silkitress version which retailed at 3/11d (19p), or the superior Silkispun wig, 4/6d (23p). Both wigs were 'brushable and combable'. She was packaged in a polythene bag with an attached header card bearing a coloured drawing of a fashionable young lady. The card stated, 'Jinx by Amanda Jane. Buy me and collect my wonderful trousseau.'

Jinx was another of those dolls sold ready to be dressed at home – the difference being that it was hoped children would purchase the ready-made clothes out of their pocket money, rather than knit for her. These tiny garments were all made in Britain by a team of outworkers, and attention to detail was impressive. Often, jackets boasted real pockets and dresses were properly lined. There were little satchels, slippers and suede boots while the felt schoolgirl and riding hats were pressed using old Luton hat forms. The catalogue boasted: 'Amanda Jane, who pioneered the idea of everything for every doll, now offers you in this catalogue some 350 items...'. As the prices of the clothing and accessories ranged from 2d upwards, even a child with just a few pennies was able to add to her Jinx collection.

Jinx by Amanda Jane

Very recently, the final demise of the Jinx dolls has come to light. Frank Strudwick, formerly of *Children's Treasures*, Hastings, purchased an assortment of 1950s moulds for doll shoes in the 1980s, which were finally scrapped in 2001, after having been used to produce thousands of Cinderella doll shoes (see Chapter 8), and it seems that amongst them were the moulds for Jinx.

Frank Strudwick said:

I am reminded of one of the many moulds we had, and can see the imprints of the two halves now, possibly Jinx. Before anyone asks, it would have been impractical to have had any more made. Even if the mould was still serviceable we would have had to buy a ton of raw material, get it shipped to the factory, who would have expected us to order 1000 dolls or more. At one time we had 30 or 40 moulds but only used about a dozen of them. They each weighed 3 or 4 cwt and were irregular shapes. This made storage a nightmare. In hindsight I wish we had kept one for historical interest but in the end we scrapped the lot. Believe me, we wouldn't have ended production if it hadn't become uneconomical to continue.

Although this was a sad fate for the beloved Jinx doll, it is interesting to know about this final episode in her life; it finishes her story. This is something we can't do with most other dolls.

Bluebox

Although not really a British company, this has been included because its little 'cheap and cheerful' hard plastic babies were available in local toy shops and newsagents, and turn up regularly today – in fact, the company is still active. Founded in 1952, by Peter Chan Pui, the first item made was a little drink and wet doll, with sleep eyes and an open mouth. The dolls were made in Hong Kong, and the brittle, thin, shiny plastic is very distinctive. Later dolls utilised a softer plastic.

Jinx by Amanda Jane

British National Dolls (BND)

Founded by E. Ainsley in London in 1928, this company, rather like *Pedigree*, was run by three brothers, initially producing china-headed and composition dolls. After the war, they switched to hard plastic. The brothers bought all their moulds from America, hence the close resemblance of *BND* dolls to classic American dolls.

Collectors know this company for their Dollie Walker large girl walking dolls, the 10 inch Babykins and the pensive-faced toddlers. The Babykins is frequently found in a shiny creamy-pink hard plastic; unfortunately, this is becoming susceptible to HPD (See Chapter 10). Later, it was issued in a matt plastic, not so pale. Babykins are jointed at the neck, shoulders and hips, and have sleep eyes or moulded hair. Often, these were sold undressed, ready to knit or sew for. Their boxes, decorated with pictures of the doll in various poses were marked, 'Babykins in different positions. Sitting, Standing, Kicking, Crawling'.

The *BND* toddler dolls stood 13 inches high and featured either moulded hair or wigs – the moulded hair version is more commonly found today. They were jointed at the neck, shoulders and hips, and featured a mama voice-box in the back. Their faces were sweet and solemn, and were often sold in lawn dresses with matching bonnets, and, like other *BND* dolls were sold through branches of Marks and Spencers.

BND Toddler

An In-Depth Look at a BND Dollie Walker

The *BND* Dollie Walker, made in the early 1950s, is an easy doll to recognise; her face, (with its open/closed mouth revealing a moulded tongue) is distinctive. Her mohair wig is styled in plaits, and the company boasted that it could be combed, waved or curled. Dollie Walker is 21 inches tall, and features sleep eyes, and a mama grille in her tummy to allow her to cry. Other easily recognisable characteristics are her rather large hands with splayed fingers. She is marked 'BND Made in England' across her back.

Dollie Walker's box and leaflets are packed with information, as well as typical 1950s graphics which show a child guiding a very large doll by the arms: 'Did you ever see a dream walking? It's a wonderful toy. It's a British National Doll product. Dollie Walker does everything. Walks, turns her head, sits, stands, sleeps, no keys, no winding.' The instructions also contain an important warning that the doll's head must not incline forward: 'To walk alongside Dollie Walker, hold her by her left or right hand. Balance Dollie Walker first on one foot then the other, just as you walk yourself. Repeat this motion as you walk,' and so on in a similar vein. The instructions also explain how to carefully push the doll's legs into a sitting position.

The Dollie Walker range wore cotton dresses, in various small prints, often with lace and buttons. They had white socks and plastic shoes. *BND* made the clothes in their factory, and in fact, later in their career, were offered a contract supplying pyjamas to Marks and Spencer, but they turned it down. Unfortunately, the majority of their dolls were sold through Marks and Spencer, and after a change of policy in 1960, the store decided they would no longer stock them. *BND* had few other outlets; they had been supplying Marks and Spencer with dolls for 33

ND Dollie alker

years. Consequently, the business rapidly declined, closing down a year later. Perhaps, had they accepted the clothing contract, they might still be in business today.

Chiltern

Though one of Britain's foremost doll producers, the world of hard plastics seem more or less to have passed this company by. Leon Rees, who worked at *Eisenmann and Company*, a major toy importers, inherited the *Chiltern Toy Works* when Joseph Eisenmann died in 1919. Leon decided to make china-headed and rubber dolls and entered into partnership with Harry Stone, formerly of *J. K. Farnell*, manufacturers of teddy bears. They developed *H. G. Stone and Company* and opened a factory in North London, using the brand name *Chiltern*.

Not long after the Second World War, *Leon Rees and Co. Ltd.* became concessionaires for the *Rosebud* dolls which were made by *Nene Plastics*, selling some of the 7 inch size hard plastic dolls under the *Chiltern* name. These small hard plastic dolls were often sold as costume dolls, dressed in costumes from many lands. They were also sold undressed for people to knit and sew for, and were featured in magazines during the 1950 and 1960s. Marked *Chiltern* on the back, they were jointed just at the shoulders; the body, head and legs being moulded in all in one. The *H.G. Stone* company moved to Pontypool, Wales, in the late 1950s, where they manufactured vinyl dolls under the *Chiltern* trademark, and produced several classics, amongst them the famed 1960s Babykins (not to be confused with the *BND* hard plastic doll of the same name). When Leon died in 1963, the companies were taken over by the *Dunbee-Combex* group, which later became a division of *Chad Valley*.

Fairylite

This company produced many doll's novelties, yet little seems to be known about it. It sold delightful dolls' glass feeding bottles in the

Fairylite 'The smallest baby in the world'

1950s, as well as small doll's house hard plastic dolls and metal and plastic dolls' house furniture. Another doll item was 'The Smallest Baby in the World', a tiny plastic baby, $3/4$ inch high, who fitted into her own little plastic bath. The company also made many other toys, including a set of *Thunderbirds* characters, and was famed for its plastic word games and puzzles. These pocket games consisted of a small square containing lettered tiles which could be rearranged to form words or designs. The *Fairylite* trademark was owned by *Graham Brothers* of Endell Street, London, and the company was originally established in the late 1800s. Just before the Second World War, it was selling celluloid dolls under the *Fairylite* name. The name was subsequently altered to *Fairylite Moulded Plastics Ltd* in the mid-1950s.

Kader

A crop of 'cheap and cheerful' dolls appeared in the mid-1950s, including a huge range made by *Kader*. Very similar, possibly even made at the same factory, were dolls marked *Evergreen*, *Agrespoly*, *Camay* and others. Although these dolls were not British, I feel they deserve a place here as they were sold throughout the country, especially in newsagents and on market stalls. The dolls continued to be made, with little change, well into the 1970s, and because

An early 1950s Kader baby doll

of their styling can appear older than they actually are.

Kader dolls are marked 'OK Kader' on their backs, together with a globe, and are made of a thin and brittle shiny plastic. They are bald-headed and range in size from tiny 3 inch babies, to 25 inches or more. Many of them feature moving tongues and twist wrists, and are very distinctive. They normally have glassene sleep eyes. Apart from the babies, often found are a range of attractive girl dolls with hair moulded into a fringed style, which gives them a 1930s appearance. There are also boy dolls with short, side-parted moulded hair and a teen range, which include some really large sizes.

It is difficult to find out much about the early days of this factory, but it was originally based in Hong Kong.

Kleeware

Founded by the Kleeman family in 1938, at first *Kleeware* concentrated on small domestic items such as combs and ashtrays, but during the war they switched to making radio components for the Ministry of Defence, as well as combs for the Forces. When hostilities ceased they resumed production of assorted domestic items - various housewares, toothbrushes, hair slides and, of course, small toys and dolls. Obviously the company was quite dynamic and go-ahead; it soon turned into a large concern with state of the art machines.

At first, *Kleeware* products were manufactured in Welwyn Garden City, using modern *American Reed Prentice* injection moulding machines, together with compression moulding machines. However the company became so successful that it needed larger premises and moved to Aycliffe, Co. Durham. Apparently, at one time, when the

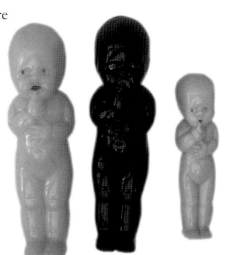

Kleeware All-in-one dolls

factory was at peak production, there were 50 injection machines installed, and 900 staff moulded and assembled a huge range of toys, including clockwork items. Other toys made by *Kleeware* included model trucks, planes, construction kits, money boxes, rattles and larger items such as toy castles, while a particularly popular line was a toy gun which fired ping-pong balls. The company also licensed to *Mettoy* the Playtown range of building kits for model railways. *Kleeware*'s housewares and toys were sold to Woolworths in great quantities, and were also exported around the world.

Kleeware's most recognisable dolls are the delightful all-in-one hard plastic babies which came in various sizes. They featured painted eyes and mouths, and had moulded hair. Each doll was sucking its right index finger. The larger sizes seem to contain beads or similar, and were sold as rattles for small children. These plastic babies came in black or white, and are marked *Kleeware* on their backs. The company also produced rubbery-plastic seated doll's house dolls with outstretched arms. They must have made these in their millions; certainly, in the 1950s, these ubiquitous babies were in every dolls house, and seemed to be on the counter of every toy shop.

Another very popular *Kleeware* line was dolls house furniture, which was sold in assorted sets during the 1950s/1960s. Kitchen sets featured all the latest mod-cons such as fridges and electric cookers; bedrooms had large wardrobes and 'knee-hole' dressing tables; bathrooms came with modern low-level suites, while lounge furniture consisted of fashionably wide armchairs, plush sofas, must-have television sets, standard lamps with pleated shades, and wonderful grand pianos complete with a stool and 'sheet music'. All were created from hard plastic, sometimes in proper 'wood' colours, but often in brighter shades. Their little rubbery dolls fitted into the *Kleeware* armchairs while the smallest size doll was perfect to be wrapped in a scrap of lace and seated on the lap of the larger doll.

When the company switched to a softer plastic in the late 1950s, they began making brightly coloured miniature prams for doll's house dolls. These cute little prams had moving hoods, and were quite robust. Inside each pram was an ingenious baby moulded all-in-one with the bedding. Similar babies fitted into *Kleeware* rocking cradles.

In 1959, *Kleeware* sold out to *Rosedale* plastics, the makers of *Tudor Rose* dolls, who were probably the company's greatest rival. By then, *Kleeware* had a flourishing raw material business and had changed direction.

Linda

Linda dolls consisted of a range of inexpensive hard plastic dolls, sold from newsagents, market stalls and similar outlets in the 1950s and 1960s. Later the makers switched to a softer vinyl, and also a rubbery plastic, which they used for such toys as Bend-A-Family bendable doll's house dolls. This was yet another Hong Kong based company, but the *Linda* dolls were of a superior plastic to those dolls from the *Kader* group of companies.

An In-Depth Look at a Linda Girl

Particularly liked by collectors are the small, $7^1/2$ inches high, girl dolls which bear a great likeness to Miss Rosebud. These dolls are easily distinguished, however, by the glossy, almost waxy, bloom. It is extremely distinctive. The *Linda* dolls were usually dressed in a frock and bonnet, either made from corduroy or a cotton print. The corduroy dresses were embroidered around the hem and on the bodice. Underneath the dresses the dolls wore a net petticoat (the dolls dressed in cotton print tended to have the petticoat attached to the

Girl dolls by Linda

dress), and white knickers. They had white socks and shoes.

Linda dolls are marked 'Made in Hong Kong' in a circle, with IN in the middle. They were usually packaged in flimsy cardboard open front boxes, and had hang tags. Often their clothing bore a *Linda* fabric label. The *Linda* trademark is distinctive with a swirly capital L.

The company also produced teen dolls and national costume dolls. The teens were 12 inches tall, and extra costumes could be purchased. The costume dolls were smaller at $7^1/2$ inches, and could be obtained dressed in the national costume of many lands, as well as an English Pearly King.

Rogark

Founded in 1950, this company was known for its small souvenir Welsh, Scottish and Sailor costume dolls. Situated in Penmaenmawr, North Wales, they called the doll line Gwyneth, and made the dolls themselves using a good quality plastic, which helps to distinguish them from many of the other tourist dolls. The hard plastic dolls – both girl and boy used the same mould – had sleep eyes, jointed arms and fixed head and legs, and were just under 7 inches high. The company also made smaller dolls, including 'bristle dolls' which 'danced' when the table they were standing on was tapped.

The dolls were carefully dressed, in Wales, in an authentic style, and, as with many costume dolls, are still very easy to find today in good condition, as they were rarely played with by

Bristle Finger-Tap dancing Welsh doll by Rogark

children. Instead, being bought as souvenirs, they tended to be stored in glass cabinets.

Sarold

The *Sarold* Manufacturing Company were based in Liverpool, on the Kirkby Trading Estate. The *Sarold* trademark for dolls was registered in 1950, and they made hard plastic types in various sizes, from tiny 3 inch size dolls to huge 25 inch tall babies. This was another company which supplied dolls to Woolworths stores, both dressed and undressed.

Probably most commonly found are the 7 inch high girl dolls, with unjointed legs; many of these were sold as costume dolls, Welsh and Scottish in particular. Frequently, the delightful flushed colouring is still present on the *Sarold* girls, which gives them a slightly old-fashioned look. The 7 inch jointed girls are also frequently seen; pretty dolls which can hold their own alongside Miss Rosebud and Jinx. All these dolls had sleep eyes, no lashes, small mouths and mohair wigs. The black versions had astrakhan hair. Another *Sarold*, popular with today's collectors, is the 25 inch bent-limbed baby. This large doll is quite light for its size, and tends to lose the colouring over the years. Often, too, the eyes fade until they are blurred.

Large Sarold baby

An In-Depth Look at a Sarold Girl

Sarold dolls were marked 'Sarold Made in England', and have a certain charisma which makes them instantly recognisable to collectors. It is surprising, given the huge quantities in which these dolls were sold and the fact that they were affordable to families on a lower budget, how few of them are around today. However, the plastic used on some of them was of a lighter mix than that used by *Tudor Rose* and other rivals, so it could be that they were broken more easily.

This pretty *Sarold* girl is 10 inches high, and is jointed at neck, shoulders and hips, all fastened with elastic. A deep groove runs around the back of each wrist. She has a rounded face, and is made of a matt plastic which is very attractive. Her face colouring is excellent, and she has sleep eyes with stiff 'paintbrush bristle' type eyelashes. She has a small open/closed mouth and rosy cheeks, and her blonde wig is made from soft mohair, styled in two plaits.

Sarold girl

Selco

Selco was owned by *MPI (Musical and Plastics Industries)*, a company which also owned *Selmer*, famed for its amplifiers and musical instruments. The *Selco* operation was based in Braintree, Essex, concentrating on plastic toys and garden furniture. In the 1960s it became well known for its toy Beatle Guitars which are widely collected today. Amongst *Selco*'s toy output was an unusual dressing-up doll. This 1950s brittle, hard plastic doll was totally flat, apart from a right-angled base so that she could stand, and featured a rather fetching cami-knicker set moulded onto her body. Her moulded brown hair was styled in a side-parted fashion with waves, and she had shoes and socks. This delightful doll came with a selection of

Selco plastic dress-up dolls with clip on plastic outfits

clip-on outfits, such as a 'fur-trimmed' coat, a buttoned pyjama (or siren suit), a long rose-trimmed gown and a short-sleeved top and skirt. All these items were flat plastic creations, and they clipped neatly onto the doll with plastic lugs, following the traditional paper doll idea. *Selco* closed in 1967.

Tudor Rose

These delightful babies and toddlers, with their serious faces, must have sold in their millions through Woolworths, as well as in toyshops. Quite cheap to buy, often sold undressed, today most collectors of British hard plastic dolls will have at least one *Tudor Rose* doll in their collection – which makes it all the more strange that scarcely anything seems to have been documented about the makers. It has proved quite difficult to discover details of the various types. *Tudor Rose* seem to have specialised in the making of small dolls, as well as numerous plastic toys.

Tudor Rose was a trademark of *Rosedale Plastics*, and the company was located in Wales from 1948 to 1978. Later, the trademark *Rosedale Rose* was used. Originally, *Rosedale/Tudor Rose* concentrated on novelties such as, buttons, combs, plastic jewellery and toys, but by the early 1950s, plastic dolls and toys were their main output. Amongst their toys was a range of hollow hard plastic toys moulded in the form of vehicles, and later they made softer, polythene-type playthings, such as a Noah's Ark. Today, *Tudor Rose* space toys are particularly sought after by collectors, as well as their trains, cars, money-boxes, and walking novelty animals. In 1971 the company was taken over, and in 1978 was purchased by *Mettoy* who sold it five years later. By then the toy output had ceased.

Tudor Rose crawling clockwork baby

An In-Depth Look at a Tudor Rose Toddler and Baby

Nowadays, the most commonly found *Tudor Rose* dolls are the small moulded-headed straight-legged babies and toddlers. These were made in two sizes and in Caucasian or black (usually more of a coffee-colour). The 8 inch versions were jointed at shoulders, head and hips, while the smaller, 6 inch dolls were jointed only at the shoulders.

The dolls were marked across their backs *Tudor Rose* and bore a rose logo, though many of the dolls sold through the Woolworths stores were unmarked with the manufacturer's name (but generally bore the wording 'Made in England'). Their sleep eyes were glassene, often featuring moulded plastic lashes. They had solemn faces, closed mouths and their distinctive hands were turned palm down. Usually the dolls are 'bald babies' with moulded hair, though occasionally they are wigged. The wigged versions seem harder to find, and beneath, like most wigged dolls of the period, is a moulded head. The vast majority seem to have been sold naked, ready to be dressed at home. Some were costumed as 'character dolls' wearing national outfits.

The smaller sized dolls were frequently dressed as fairies, often at home, perfect for adorning the top of a Christmas tree, and they

Tudor Rose baby and toddler

were also sold in boxed play-sets (such as a bath complete with soap, brush and bath-rack). (See Chapter 8.) It would be interesting to know where the moulds originated, as other little dolls, such as those made by *Sarold* and by *Ideal*, bear a strong resemblance to the *Tudor Rose* babies. It is likely that the company, like so many other 1950s concerns, obtained the moulds from America.

Blondy Blueyes by Tudor Rose

The most distinctive *Tudor Rose* doll was a walking girl with a moulded plastic dress, similar to one made by *Roddy*, though larger. The *Tudor Rose* walker was called Blondy Blueyes and stood 7 inches high. Blondy Blueyes had sleep eyes, and she didn't have a proper lower body – her legs were fastened to a plastic bar under her skirt. As she walked, her head turned from side to side. Blondy Blueyes' dress came in assorted colours; yellow and blue are most commonly seen, and her box was marked *Rosedale Plastics*.

The *Tudor Rose* company also made a range of small, delightful hard-plastic doll accessories such as a wash tub with a mangle and scrubbing board, and a highchair, complete with removable potty. A bright array of primary colours was used for these toys – very typical of the 1950s. In those days companies were so gratified with the way plastics could easily be dyed, that they tended to use colour as much as they could.

UP

Little is known about this company, which produced its dolls in Hong Kong, but it is included here as the dolls were attractive, innovative and very popular. Most often seen are a range of 12 inch teen girls, marked *UP* on their backs. These dolls, made from a good quality hard plastic, have a rather superior look, with sleep eyes featuring plastic lashes, red rosebud-shaped mouths, short curly hair and very elegant long curved fingers topped with re-painted nails. The dolls were usually sold in a plastic bra and silky pants, ready to be dressed at home, and were quite a novelty when first introduced as they were very affordable and glamorous. Probably sold through smaller toyshops and market stalls in the 1950s, but by the 1960s they were sold in plastic packaging through Tesco Home and Wear stores, amongst other outlets.

Teen doll marked 'UP'

Wells/Brimtoy

This company, based in Walthamstow, East London, was renowned for its clockwork tinplate goods, especially toys such as trainsets, buses, trams and cars. However, it did produce a few items of interest to the doll collector. It was founded in the 1920s in Somers Road, as *A Wells and Co.* Later, Brimtoy joined Wells and they moved to larger premises in Stirling Road, Walthamstow, where the company was more than able to hold its own against the German tinplate toy manufacturers. Its registered trademark was of *Nelson's Column*. The factory closed in 1965.

The Dancing Clockwork Cinderella and Prince Charming toy, sold as Novelty Mechanical Waltzing Figures, can still be found easily. This delightful pair of dancers features Cinderella in a sparkly moulded gown, usually pale blue, and her Prince, who wears a smart military uniform. When wound, the dancing pair rotate. Dating from the early 1950s, they are also found in other colourways. Other *Wells/Brimtoy* doll-type items include a Fairy Godmother, a Spanish Dancer and Mary Had a Little Lamb. This last doll trails the lamb behind her, from a hook attached to her dress. These delightful moving dolls were made from a rather brittle plastic, with a metal clockwork mechanism, and make interesting additions to a collection of doll automata.

Clockwork dancing dolls by Wells/Brimtoy

By the late 1950s, softer vinyl was taking over from hard plastics (see Chapter 7) and in the 1960s few hard plastic dolls were made. The hard plastic doll era had lasted for just 10 years, yet this golden age had produced dozens of different types of beautiful and innovative dolls. Hard plastic dolls had a certain charm which vinyl has never been able to fully recapture.

Tudor Rose Dutch Girl

Chapter 6

Not Just Plastics

Dolls were not just made of plastic in the 1950s – other substances were used too, such as rubber, paper, composition and cloth. Additionally, there was a much softer, rubbery kind of pvc, similar to but not quite the same as the product later developed to become vinyl. Some kinds of vinyl had a softer, squidgy feel, so that, too, is included here, even though purists will no doubt feel it should be listed in the plastics section! Also under this heading comes the small, soft rubber/PVC squeaky toys sold for babies and toddlers, which were often in the shape of dolls as well as all kinds of creatures. In fact, I have included here any plastics which I feel do not fall into the category of 'vinyl' as the general doll collector understands it, ie; a firm, matt, thick, yielding kind of plastic, but not rubbery, sticky, thin or very soft.

Cloth Dolls

The traditional medium for dolls has always been cloth, and the 1950s were no exception. Cloth dolls, especially for younger children, were comforting to hold and perfect for snuggling up to at night. Very popular at the time were the so called 'Baby Bunting' dolls. These very basic unjointed colourful cloth dolls had faces made from stiffened muslin, moulded card, celluloid or thin plastic. The faces were either glued or sewn onto the front of the cloth head. Often, the top of the head was tapered to a point, at other times it was rounded. Cloth manufacturers of the decade included *Dean's* and *Chad Valley*.

Unmarked cloth doll with composition face

Chad Valley

The name *Chad Valley* was a well respected toy brand in the 1950s. It had first appeared on toys just after the First World War, and was actually a new name for a Victorian printing company. It had begun when a printer, Anthony Bunn Johnson, decided to make simple picture games for children as a sideline, then, in 1860, his two sons Joseph and Alfred set up a business called Johnson Brothers in Birmingham, concentrating on stationery. 37 years later, the company moved to a valley near the River Chad, at Harborne, on the outskirts of Birmingham, which later inspired the name, *Chad Valley*.

This company produced many different dolls and soft toys, at first at Harborne and later at Wellington, Staffordshire. One of the first ranges was a set of printed stockinette dolls with hand-woven wigs. Soon, they began to experiment with new materials such as celluloid, developing an excellent reputation for quality and attention to detail. Perhaps the most famous of their earlier dolls were the Snow White and Seven Dwarfs set of the 1930s, and the later Mabel Lucie Attwell dolls.

After the war, the company resumed doll production, continuing into the early 1950s with dolls such as a schoolgirl, nurse and soldier, but gradually, the dolls lost popularity as plastics came into their own. Eventually, children regarded the cloth dolls as old-fashioned and *Chad Valley* increasingly turned its attention to soft toys and teddy bears, receiving a welcome boost when Harry Corbett lost hold of his puppet, Sooty, on a live television programme. The slip revealed a *Chad Valley* identity label on the puppet and sales of Sooty soared. Eventually the *Chad Valley* name was sold to Woolworths.

Dean's plush Ronnie doll

Dean's Ragbook Company

The *Dean's Ragbook Company* was formed in 1903, and by the 1920s was producing a range of cloth dolls. One of the company's most famed dolls was the delightful Betty Oxo from the 1930s, an advertising doll obtainable with a quantity of tokens saved from Oxo cube packets. By the 1950s the company was making beautifully-moulded rubber-headed dolls on jointed cloth bodies. As well as an enchanting range of girl dolls, with names such as Lucy, Nancy, Joan, Vivian and Beryl, there were a pair of Dutch dolls, a Chinese boy and girl (Ting Ling and Hu Rang) and Annie and Buffalo Billy, who were a cowgirl and cowboy. Annie cost 27/6d (£1.38), while Buffalo Billy was a snip at 19/- (88p). There was also a plush-bodied doll called Ronnie, who first appeared just before the war, and proved so popular that he survived well into the 1950s. The Coronation gave rise to a collection of patriotic dolls (See Chapter 2). As *Chad Valley* had discovered, the demand for soft dolls was waning, and *Dean*'s primarily switched to soft toys and bears, just issuing a few token dolls from time to time.

Old Cottage

The Fleischmann family arrived in Britain in 1938 after fleeing Czechoslovakia, and later settled at Rustington, near Littlehampton, West Sussex. Sadly, Margaret Fleischmann was soon widowed, and she began to make dolls for a living, registering the name *Old Cottage Toys* in 1939. Initially, the dolls were made from cloth, with cloth masks, but by the early 1950s the dolls were being made using a mix of PVA and latex rubber for the heads, which gave them

Old Cottage cloth girl

a highly distinctive look, attached to jointed cloth bodies. The heads of the *Old Cottage* dolls were hand-painted and the costumes were all designed by Margaret Fleischmann, while much of the sewing was executed by outworkers. All the outfits were beautifully made, and the final overseeing of every doll was carried out by Margaret before it was declared ready for dispatch. *Old Cottage Toys* continued production up until 1980 – pretty, dainty dolls still very much collected today.

Composition

As we have already seen (Chapters 1 & 2) composition was still very much alive and well in the 1950s, particularly during the first half of the decade. In fact, as late as 1956, my mother bought me a composition doll for my birthday from the market in St. Albans. I called the doll Elizabeth and she was always one of my favourites. I'm pleased to say I still have her. She is 18 inches high, with a 'tanned look' complexion and orange lips. She is marked FP on the back of her neck, which I believe stands for Frank Popper, a prolific 1940s/1950s doll maker. Certainly, these 'bronze toned' dolls are very easy to find and are extremely distinctive. They are made of a pot-type composition, often white on the inside and sharp if broken. My Elizabeth doll has sleep eyes, a mama unit in her back, and is jointed with thick elastic at neck, hips and shoulders.

It is quite difficult to date composition dolls, as many are unmarked, but it seems that a range of large dolls were popular as fairground and carnival prizes in the early 1950s, and there are some lovely examples still to be found.

Author's FP childhood composition doll, known as 'Elizabeth', bought 1956

Also, of course, many children owned composition dolls bought for them during or immediately after the war. Many of these wartime dolls are of a very poor quality with crudely painted features – but it is well to remember that at the time they would have been well loved, and may have been a child's only comfort. Some of these would have accompanied children through frightening air raids in dark shelters.

Paper/Card

Paper dolls have long been popular. The name is something of a misnomer, as the doll is normally made from card. However, the clothing is invariably made from paper, with small tabs on the shoulders and sides of garments, enabling them to be folded over and fixed to the doll. Dolls such as these were made by many companies, often book publishers, and sold in bookshops, newsagents, 'corner shops' and market stalls. Ephemera of this kind is invariably short-lived, so it is a bonus when a collector comes across an early paper doll and her garments. One 1950s company which deserves a mention is *Philmar*, as their paper dolls were a little more unusual than most.

Unmarked 1950s composition doll

Philmar

Philmar Ltd were based in London, and were especially famed for their huge range of jigsaw puzzles and games. However, they also made a series of dressing-up dolls, some of which featured 'real hair'. The delightful dolls include a fairy princess, and 'Elaine and Vicki Darling Dolls with wavy hair'. These 9 inch high dolls were well made from stout card and they came with six printed paper sheets of outfits ready for cutting out. Their wigs were made from very soft mohair. The company also made Magnetic Joan whose card body held a concealed magnet. Her clothes had metal strips to help them magically attach to the doll.

Philmar paper dolls

Rubber/Latex/Beauty Skin/Magic Skin

Newfeld Ltd. (Bendy Toys)

Not strictly dolls, perhaps, but included here partly because of their unusual construction and partly because they were responsible for a particularly popular baby toy in the 1950s, Bendy Baby, a premium made for Fairy soap. Fairy soap used a picture of a baby in a fluffy towelling nappy, with a little quiff of hair, on their soap packets, and the foam rubber doll was intended to represent that baby. The soft, cuddly toys were made of foam rubber over a wire armature, which allowed the figures to be posed in many different ways. *Bendy Toys* was owned by Charles Neufeld, who called the manufacturing company

Neufeld Ltd. The company began in London before moving to Ashford, Middlesex in the early 1950s.

Apparently, the Americans were particularly taken with the toys but initially, high export tariffs meant that the company could not compete with larger manufacturers by keeping the price low. They attempted to manufacture the toys in the United States, but that was unworkable because Charles Neufeld lacked the resources to compete with US manufacturers – dealers in the US expected far larger mark ups than was usual in Britain. As far as I know, the company are still in business.

Pedigree 'Beauty Skin'

Pedigree Beauty Skin dolls first appeared in the late 1940s, and were popular until the mid-1950s. They were registered in 1948, by *Pedigree Soft Toys Ltd* and were pretty dolls, mostly with hard plastic heads. Bodies were made from a thin latex rubber skin stuffed with kapok. Smaller children, especially, were fond of them as they were soft to cuddle, apart from the hard head. However they did have drawbacks, the latex skin tended to disintegrate – it would either split or rot – when that happened the white kapok stuffing would ooze from the doll. The arms and legs were particularly vulnerable, and would wither away. Although the instructions, which came with the dolls, explained how they must be regularly powdered, this was not always adhered to, and so they soon cracked and split, presumably from a combination of rough handling, washing, sweaty hands and general wear and tear. Many of those which do survive have badly damaged arms and legs, and have usually been covered with sticking plaster to keep the split edges together. A Beauty Skin doll in good condition is a very rare find today.

When I was little, my favourite doll was one of these Beauty Skin babies, made by *Pedigree*, and I called her Jeannie. Sadly, she began to wither until she couldn't be played with any more. One day she 'disappeared', presumably to the dustbin. Although I had other dolls,

Author with her favourite Beauty Skin, early 1950s

I missed her, and so when I was asked what I would like for Christmas – I must have been about six – I asked for another soft doll, just like Jeannie. I found Isabelle on Christmas morning, wearing a white satin dress and lying in a little blue-draped metal crib. I loved Isabelle dearly, and I had her for many years, even though her right arm slowly, but completely, disintegrated. However, her body didn't split at all, and neither did her legs. Much of the damage was no doubt caused by too much love – the warmth of a child's arms affected the thin rubber. Also, any small knock or graze could rupture the skin. Water damaged the doll, too – it needed to be thoroughly dried and powdered after getting wet; sadly, these lovely dolls were just too vulnerable.

They were made in four sizes, though the smallest didn't have a hard plastic head, but one made from rubber – which presumably made for a more cuddly doll. The hard plastic headed versions were 14 inches, 16 inches and 20 inches, and the *Pedigree* catalogue for 1955 contained mentions of several different versions. Though most featured 'moulded heads' with delicate curls, a girl with a 'brushable hair' wig was also available. There was a choice of outfits for all the different Beauty Skin varieties - a child could choose from romper, dress, sunsuit or long gown. At the time the retail price for a plastic-headed Beauty Skin began at 18/11d for a 14 inch version 'with napkin', while 16 ins dolls began at 28/6d and 20 inch versions from 36/3d upwards, depending on the outfits. Many parents would settle on the cheapest, 18/6d version, and then dress the doll themselves.

Over the years, when talking to other doll collectors, I've found that the Beauty Skin doll is often remembered with great affection. It's the one which so many search for, as they all experienced the same feeling of loss when their own Beauty Skin baby withered away when they were small. Although I have since acquired many lovely dolls, my most pleasurable acquisition was a Beauty Skin doll which I obtained a few years ago. My daughter suddenly came across her, almost perfect, when we visited an antiques centre and bought her over to show me in triumph, knowing that I had wanted one for so long.

An In-Depth Look at a Pedigree Beauty Skin

This rare doll measures 16 inches tall, and has sleeping, flirty eyes. She has a delicately modelled face, small nose, and red lips set in a slight smile. Her head is made from hard plastic and her hair is moulded with curls framing her face. She is marked, 'Pedigree, England' on the nape of her neck.

Her body is firmly stuffed below the thin layer of rubber and contains a mama unit, hidden behind a diamond shaped grid of 16 holes. It issues a two-note cry, 'mama' when the doll is tipped. Her legs are also firmly stuffed with kapok and covered with the thin rubber, while her arms are similarly constructed (though they feel softer). The doll's hands appear quite large, owing to the construction – each finger is separately stuffed with kapok. The 1953 *Pedigree* catalogue depicts Beauty Skin dolls as being sold in various outfits such as a locknit sunsuit, silk romper, long frilled gown, or dress made of Inglewave, silk or printed organdie.

The 1955 catalogue lists a 10

**Pedigree Beauty Skin,
very rare**

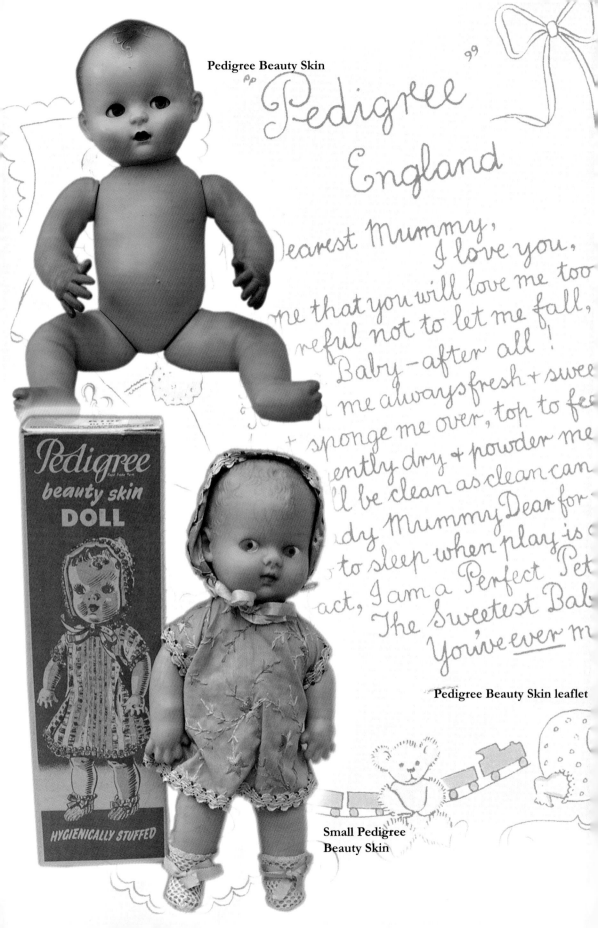

Pedigree Beauty Skin

"Pedigree" England

Dearest Mummy,
I love you,
...me that you will love me too
...reful not to let me fall,
Baby — after all!
...me always fresh + swee...
+ sponge me over, top to fe...
...ently dry + powder me
...'ll be clean as clean can
...dy Mummy Dear for...
...to sleep when play is
...act, I am a Perfect Pet
The Sweetest Bab...
You've ever m...

Pedigree Beauty Skin leaflet

Pedigree beauty skin DOLL
HYGIENICALLY STUFFED

Small Pedigree Beauty Skin

inch Beauty Skin doll with a 'delightful baby's layette . . . presented in a completely upholstered Winkie Crib completely enclosed in cellophane'. This Winkie Crib fastened at each end with press studs, so could be opened out completely flat if required.

Beauty Skin Dolls came with a delightful, 'hand-written' leaflet which read:

> *My Dearest Mummy, I love you,*
> *I hope that you will love me too.*
> *Be careful not to let me fall,*
> *I am a Baby - after all!*
> *To keep me always fresh and sweet,*
> *Just sponge me over, top to feet,*
> *Then gently dry and powder me,*
> *And I'll be clean as clean can be,*
> *I'm ready Mummy Dear for fun,*
> *And go to sleep when play is done.*
> *In fact I am a Perfect Pet,*
> *The sweetest Babe you've ever met.*

The smaller, 9 inch version, had a moulded vinyl head with painted plastic eyes. Her Beauty Skin body and limbs were made from soft 'washable latex rubber.' The *Pedigree* doll box says, 'Made in England International Model Aircraft Ltd, Merton, London' and points out that the doll is 'hygienically stuffed'.

Other companies issued their own versions of Beauty Skin, such as *Palitoy* who made Petal Skin.

Petal Skin (Palitoy)

Palitoy created their Petal Skin dolls in 1956, using a soft vinyl for the body and limbs, which was often stuffed with a hygienic filling. As

Palitoy Petal Skin

with the *Pedigree* dolls, the larger versions had hard plastic heads while the smaller kinds had soft moulded heads.

They bore labels which stated:

Your new dolly will get as soiled as you during the playtime hours. Wash it as carefully as you do yourself, using soap and water. No harm can come to your Vinyl petal skin doll and to have clean playthings is hygienic.

Should the blush on the face become faint from constant washing, a little rouge will soon restore those rosy cheeks. Take good care of your new playmate.

An In-Depth Look at a Palitoy Petal skin

This little boy measures 12 inches high. He is made from a vinyl/plastic which feel rubbery, and is very soft to touch. His hair is beautifully moulded, with curls and a side parting, and his head and limbs are attached with a push joint fitting, very similar to the *Mormit* dolls (see *Mormit* entry in this chapter). He has fixed plastic eyes, in this case, lilac, a colour much-favoured by *Palitoy*, and he has an open/closed mouth with his lips coloured a pale pink.

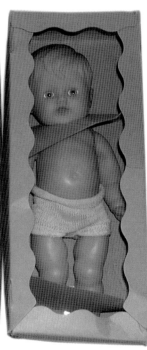

Palitoy Petal Skin boy

Palitoy Petal Skin girl

The hands and feet are nicely molded with great attention to detail – knuckles, nails and dimples are all meticulously marked out, and he wears a pair of cotton pants, ready to be dressed at home. He was sold packaged in a polythene bag inside a sturdy yellow *Palitoy* box, complete with the usual 'I am a Vinyl Petal-skin Doll. Flexible, Washable, Unbreakable.' He also has a *Palitoy* gold swing tag.

The *Palitoy* dolls did not seem to disintegrate as often the *Pedigree* ones did, consequently, they are much more easy to find today. Some of the larger models were dressed in colourful plastic dresses and matching bonnets, which, over the years, have grown very stiff, almost brittle. Presumably, at the time no one realised that the properties of plastic would alter over the years. (See Chapter 10).

An In-Depth Look at a Palitoy Patsy

This was one of the early drink and wet dolls, and proved very popular. Made by *Palitoy* in 1950, the head was made from a rubbery kind of plastic. She has moulded hair, fixed glassene eyes and an open mouth to take a bottle or dummy. Distinctive seams run along her arms, and her fingers are fused together. A few years later she was updated and given a hard plastic head, with a more 'o' shaped mouth, and later still was updated to a softer version made from a form of PVC.

An early 1950s advert for Patsy claimed she was a 'Sensational New Novelty':

I'm almost human in my accomplishments. I talk, I go to sleep, I cry real tears, I feed from my bottle, I blow bubbles. I'm a pretty girl, 15 inches tall, almost unbreakable and you can wash and powder me as much as you like. I come to you safely packed in a strong colourful box which

Early version of Patsy by Palitoy

makes into a rocking cradle, with nappy, pins, feeding bottle, comforter and
bubble pipe. I cost 42/- postage 1/6'.

The advert was placed by Sydney Ross, who had various showrooms around London and the South-east.

Palitoy continued to experiment with various plastics, and the company particularly came into its own in the 1960s and 1970s with a huge range of innovative dolls.

Mormit Rubber-type PVC

The distinctive, rubbery-feel *Mormit* dolls were first produced by the *F. G. Mitchell* company in 1945, and were so durable that they are easily found today, though often are slightly discoloured. The compound used for the dolls was trialled by *F. G. Mitchell* in a domestic oven in a bungalow in Chingford, using a mould formed from an existing 1940s doll and made from plaster of Paris. The doll which emerged from that oven was created from a new material called polyvinyl chloride, or PVC.

The greatest innovation was that the arms, legs and head were attached to the body by a special flange, meaning that for the first time dolls did not need to be strung. This construction of the *Mormit* dolls meant that children could bathe them safely, without fear of them softening, disolving or flaking, as used to happen to the composition dolls. Now, not only could the dolls get wet without harm, their push-fit construction meant that the limbs could be removed to allow the dolls to drain, thus avoiding the problem of rotting (which often happened to rubber dolls). These practical, child-friendly dolls must have been a boon to parents. As the dolls dried off relatively quickly, it saved the problem of wet leaky dolls, which could take days to dry out.

Mormit Marie Valerie

Naturally, the *F.G. Mitchell* company took out patents to cover the construction of the dolls, as well as the manufacture of the eye-sockets and the mechanism. Apparently, it seems that *Cascelloid* (later known as *Palitoy*), must have been working on a similar idea, and they applied for similar patents. However, the two companies seemed to have come to some agreement, as there was no dispute.

Mormit dolls are surprisingly heavy, and they have bald heads with moulded hair and rather basic features. The dolls' eyes vary, the earliest were glass – later glassene - and then they were composite transfer-printed with a clear lens over the top. Sometimes the dolls have open mouths and were of the drink and wet type, with a rubber tube mechanism inside. Not generally known is that they originally had a voice – they squeaked! The squeaks rarely lasted for long, maybe water affected them when they were bathed. When the dolls left the factory they had painted faces, but nowadays they are normally found with the paint worn away. Over the years, the dolls tend to turn a strange brown colour, caused by handling and sweat. It is also due to the fact that the dyes used in the pvc at the time weren't colourfast.

F. G. Mitchell called the dolls Marie, adding on the names of his daughters as a second name. The first two dolls were Marie Jose and Marie Valerie, which stood 9 inch and 13 inch respectively, and were produced in 1945, just after the war. They must have been some of the earliest of the pre-war dolls. A year later, along came Marie Mia (11 inch) and Marie Lou (15 inch). The largest, Marie Ann, (24 inch) was produced for the maternity services, and was used to demonstrate to trainee midwives how to handle and bath a baby. This doll was meant to resemble a nine-month old child.

Mormit dolls could be taken apart to drain out water

During 1948/49, three more dolls joined the *Mormit* family – Prince Charming, Baby Prince Charming and Princess Linda. The two princes were similar to the Marie series, with the standard bald head and push on limbs, but Princess Linda was completely different. Her body was a latex skin stuffed with flock or ground latex, though her head was PVC – she is exceedingly rare nowadays. She presumably was of similar construction to the *Pedigree* Beauty Skin. Princess Linda was the only *Mormit* doll which was sold dressed, and was also the only *Mormit* doll not to have been produced in a black version. Black versions of *Mormit* dolls were made to order, most going to South Africa and the West Indies, and are fairly hard to find today.

The take-apart construction proved a great selling point. It seems that during the early 1950s the managing director of *Mormit* took the dolls to a trade fair, but the wholesalers were reluctant to buy – until he scooped up an armful of the dolls, marched outside and proceeded to throw them under the wheels of the passing traffic. Open-mouthed, the buyers looked on and were astounded when the director then gathered up the doll pieces and reassembled them. The company sold three years' production in two hours!

F. G. Mitchell/Mormit also manufactured Wendy dolls, which were 6 inch-high teens made from PVC, as well as pixies, balls, ducks and fishes, and were also responsible for creating the very first plastic dart flight. The *F. G. Mitchell* companies had several factories, including some overseas; many dolls were made in other lands. However, all *Mormit* dolls are clearly marked, both with the company name and the name of the doll. Often, they bear a code letter on the neck, an indication of the factory.

An In-Depth Look at a Mormit Marie-Mia

This Marie-Mia doll produced by *F. G. Mitchell* is 11 inch high, and is marked *Mormit* Marie-Mia on her back. She is a drink and wet doll, and was sold with an opaque, boat-shaped feeding bottle moulded from a similar rubbery substance to the doll. As this one is unused,

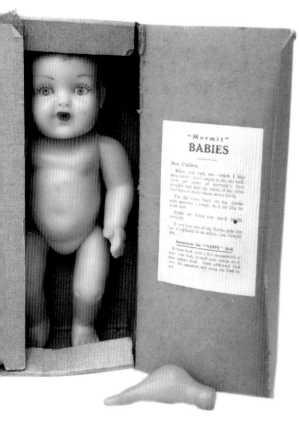

Mormit Marie-Mia Nappy Doll. Mint in box with feeding bottle

her face-paint is still perfect – hair, eyelashes, brows and lips soon rubbed off of the *Mormit* dolls, which is why the majority found today are almost featureless.

Just like other dolls in the series, her head, arms and legs could be easily removed from her body to allow water drainage. She is quite heavy for her size and contains a squeaker, which was pre-sumably meant to sound like a baby crying.

This doll was sold as a 'Nappy Feeding and Wetting Doll', and originally cost 21/6d (£1.12p.) The instructions make fascinating reading:

Dear Children

When you bath me - which I like very much - don't forget to dry me well then get some of mummy's face powder and dust the joints of my arms and legs to make them move easily.

Put the roses back on my cheeks with mummy's rouge, as I do like to look nice. Shade me from too much bright sunlight.

If you lose one of my limbs, you can get it replaced from where you bought me.

Instructions for 'Nappy' Doll:

Remove head, pour a few teaspoons of water into body to well soak cotton wool, then replace head. Each additional feed after this operation will cause the doll to wet.

Mormit dolls, such as the Nappy Doll were packed in sturdy boxes, and these boxes were made by the resourceful *Mitchell* company at their factory in Dalston. Some of the boxes were very attractive, whilst others were quite plain with simple lettering. All the doll production was done by hand but eventually ceased because the company couldn't keep up with the larger concerns. By the mid-1960s, the *F. G. Mitchell* company were concentrating on household items.

Rubber-feel Plastic (Rosebud And Others)

Rosebud was just one of the many companies producing rubber/soft plastic dolls for toddlers and squeaky dolls for babies. The squeaky dolls deserve a mention as they turn up quite frequently and are very pretty, with a distinctive vanilla smell.

The larger, heavy, moulded, rubbery, vinyl types of dolls for toddlers and older children often featured moulded ponytails. Sometimes there was a hole through the plastic where a ribbon could be tied. Many of these moulded all-in-one dolls are unmarked so it is difficult to tell the difference between the products of the various companies, which included *Palitoy*, *Pedigree* and *Roddy*. Often these dolls were sold undressed, and patterns crop up in women's magazines of the period, as well as in knitting leaflets.

Rosebud rubbery vinyl squeaky doll

Chapter 7

Vinyl Revolution

By the late 1950s, it was obvious that vinyl was the in thing for doll-making. Not only was it unbreakable, it was soft, so ideal for a doll intended to be cuddled. Vinyl could be washed without harm, and it was cheaper to manufacture – once the necessary machinery was purchased – but the most important thing of all was that the dolls' heads could be 'rooted' with nylon. This meant that however often the hair was washed, it wouldn't come unglued, unlike old-fashioned mohair wigs. It could be combed and brushed constantly without coming to harm – hair didn't fall out when it became entangled in the comb – and it could also be styled easily, without tangling. Now dolls could have all manner of hair styles, and there was no danger of them suddenly turning bald, unlike the hard plastic dolls.

However, the machinery for the new-fangled vinyl was very expensive, and most British companies couldn't afford to just discard their old machines and buy the necessary new ones. So they had to compromise. As the most important part of a doll was the head, they concentrated on making heads from vinyl. The cost must have been exorbitant, as not only did they have to buy the actual machines, they had to invest in the appliances

Rosebud hard plastic (left) and transitional version (right) knee-joint dolls

for rooting the hair, as well as, often, new moulds – *and* they had to train the workers how to use them. Some manufacturers, such as *BND*, hung on to the very end producing their hard plastic dolls (although they did make some vinyl dolls) whilst others, such as *Roddy*, were much quicker off the mark. A few companies, including *Palitoy* and *Mormit*, had been experimenting with PVC (polyvinyl chloride) since the 1940s.

When vinyl was developed, the *Roddy* company was one of the first to embrace the new medium. There were a few teething troubles at first, such as the problem of stabilising the vinyl because it had a tendency to change colour, but once these problems were overcome, a charming range of dolls rolled off the production line. Mohair could no longer be used for doll's hair, as it was unable to be rooted by machine, and many of the earlier vinyl *Roddy* dolls had saran hair, which was a man-made fibre rather coarse to touch but which could hold its style excellently, and was particularly suited to the fashionable curls of the day. As with other companies of the time, sometimes the dolls had vinyl heads and hard-plastic bodies.

Roddy dolls, produced by the *D. G. Todd* company, used an excellent, firm quality vinyl, and this is no doubt why so many *Roddy* dolls still survive in good condition today. Unfortunately there was one design weakness, which most *Roddy* collectors will have experienced; the dolls' eyes had an annoying tendency to slip from their little plastic lugs. Then the eyes could easily be pushed in or slipped round in their sockets, resulting in many wall-eyed dolls turning up today. Normally, the eyes can be repositioned by the skilful use of a pair of tweezers, though you do need a steady hand. When they are back in place, they often need a dab of glue to hold the eyes in place on the lugs, otherwise they will soon slip back round.

Roddy transitional girl

Strangely, the *Roddy* vinyl dolls don't always bear the *Roddy* name, although they usually have the words 'Made in England' printed in a circle, on their backs. Many *Roddy* dolls were produced in very large sizes, the size of a toddler or older baby, and these were often used as mannequins to model garments in the windows of baby shops, replacing the earlier plaster or china babies. It is interesting to note that although the company was one of the first to use the new technology, some of the *Roddy* hard plastic dolls were not immediately discontinued, many being made until well into the 1960s (as were the smaller *Pedigree* dolls). Other companies, too, continued to make small hard plastic dolls, especially those sold as costume dolls.

Transitionals

While the change-over from hard plastic to softer vinyl was being made, factories couldn't just waste the components they already had. In addition, they couldn't afford to replace all the machinery at once, so they often compromised by making vinyl heads. We call these dolls 'transitionals'. This is a look at a few transitional dolls of the period. Sometimes similar moulds to the hard plastic face moulds were used, while at other times new moulds were obtained.

An In-Depth Look at a Palitoy Transitional Marcher

This doll, to all intents and purposes, is very similar to the hard plastic version described in Chapter 4. She stands 20 inches tall, and is jointed at neck, shoulders and hips. Her body is made from hard plastic and features a mama unit. The tummy of this doll is much slimmer and does not have the pronounced bulge of the earlier model. The body is marked, 'Prov. Pat. 13313/50'. The hands are slightly more delicate and the fingers not quite so splayed as the hard plastic model.

However, the head is completely different to the earlier doll; it is made from a soft, almost rubbery, vinyl, and is not marked at all. The eyes are sleep eyes, rather than the flirty eyes of the hard plastic version, and the open/closed mouth reveals a neat row of upper teeth and a tongue. The colouring is very attractive, the lips being a light red while the cheeks have a pink flush. Instead of the mohair wig, this doll has short rooted curly hair made from a fairly coarse saran nylon. She still features the same marching action – when her legs are moved, her head moves from side to side while her arms move up and down.

Palitoy transitional Marcher

Rosebud, too, soon embraced the new product; and, as with other companies of the time, they realised the tremendous advantage of adopting the soft vinyl – it solved the problem of dolls losing their hair after prolonged brushing and handling and it was shatterproof. At last the hair could be securely sewn to the scalp. The saran held its style well, and they discovered that it was especially good for short bubble cuts. At this time (the late 1950s) most *Rosebud* dolls featured this shorter curly hair. Children could wash and comb saran as easily as they could their own.

Rosebud used the vinyl heads on many of their hard plastic bodies including their knee jointed dolls, utilising a similar mould to the hard plastic slight smile face. The bodies of these knee-jointed dolls were identical to the hard plastic varieties. The 1957 *Rosebud* catalogue emphasised the fact that the dolls now had 'Rooted Saran Hair' and could 'Sit, Stand and Walk'. The dolls were dressed in dresses made from taffeta, pique or printed cotton, often trimmed with braid or lace.

An In-Depth Look at a Rosebud Transitional Knee-bend

This *Rosebud* stands 17 inches tall and her body is identical to the doll in Chapter 4. However, her head has been made from a soft vinyl, which feels quite squashy, and on the back of her neck is marked *Rosebud* in script. Her hair has been rooted directly into her scalp, so now it can be combed and brushed with no fear of it coming out, unless really roughly handled. The hair is made from nylon saran, which feels rather coarse, certainly when compared to the soft mohair worn by the hard plastic-headed girl.

She has sleep eyes with long lashes, the same delicate slightly smiley mouth, and nicely painted lower lashes, which are longer than you might expect. Her body features soft pink blushing on the back of her hands and the front of her knees, and she can kneel and sit properly in a chair.

Rosebud transitional knee-joint girl

Late 1950s Vinyl Dolls

By the late 1950s, most of the doll companies were producing at least some of their range as all-vinyl dolls, realising that this was the way forward. Already, children were asking for dolls made from vinyl, preferring them to the hard plastic types, which was quite understandable – it was distressing to know that, if dropped, a favourite hard plastic doll might crack or shatter. Vinyl dolls could truly be regarded as unbreakable, as well as washable and unlikely to suddenly shed their hair due to over enthusiastic brushing.

Pedigree was just one of the companies who enthusiastically took up the new vinyl product, and by 1957 their catalogue was featuring many all-vinyl dolls, though the company continued to make many of the established hard plastic favourites, including Saucy Walkers and Pretty Peepers.

Pedigree Tender-Tex girl

The catalogue stated:

New, revolutionary Vinyl dolls are the highlights of the fabulous Pedigree range for 1957. They join an already unlimited choice of dolls ranging from six to twenty-eight inches high: including life like walking and talking dolls, baby dolls, story book characters, and many others beautifully dressed in fashionable styles.

All-vinyl dolls from the *Pedigree* company included a selection of 12 inch high walkers (with heads which turned from side to side), larger 17 inch girls and Little Miss Vogue, a $10^1/2$ inch teen doll who came with her own carry case containing various outfits. They also introduced Tender-Tex, a brand name for many of their all-vinyl babies, girl and boy dolls at this time. Tender-Tex dolls were usually sold in a polythene bag with a header card, rather than a box. Little Princess (see Chapter 2) was reissued as a 15 inch vinyl doll with 'ash blonde rooted saran hair in bubble-cut style.' She continued to wear her 'beautiful dress in best quality printed taffeta with lace frilling, specially designed by Norman Hartnell.'

Another interesting trend was the introduction of teenage dolls, with curvy figures, waists and busts. These dolls wore the fashions of the day, at first quite formal, with shirt-waisted dresses, pearl necklaces, duster coats and matching hats. Many were rather sophisticated in fur stoles and strapless evening dresses. These teens were issued by companies such as *Pedigree*, *Roddy*, *Chiltern* and *Rosebud*, and were often quite large, around 15 – 20 inches. They normally featured short hair, often in a fashionable bubblecut, and sported seamed stockings, eyeshadow, painted finger nails and toenails, earrings in their pieced ears and had arched feet to suit strappy sandals. Their heyday was the late 1950s and early 1960s, before the smaller, slimmer Barbie and Sindy ousted them.

Chapter 8

Patterns and Accessories

In the 1950s, there was still a feeling of 'make do and mend', left over from the war. People didn't throw things away – recycling, thought so innovative today, was highly popular in the 1950s.

Fabrics and wool were especially valuable. Old jumpers were painstakingly unravelled, and the wool then steamed over a kettle of boiling water, before being rewound into skeins. Children's clothes were passed down through a family, and once they were beyond repair, were cut up for dusters, cleaning cloths or rags for wiping dirty hands. Of course, all this frugality and 'making things' filtered down to the children. Girls were all taught to knit and sew, both at home and at school, and in many cases, boys were taught too.

Dolls To Dress

Lots of dolls were sold unclothed for home dressing, and doll knitting and sewing patterns were not only sold separately, but appeared in all the popular women's magazines of the day. Magazines such as *Woman*, *Woman's Weekly* and *Woman and Home* regularly included patterns, often accompanied by special offers for dolls. Probably the most famous of the dolls were the *Woman's Weekly* Twins, who were a pair of small, 7 inch, *Rosebud* dolls which appeared in all kinds of outfits. These little dolls, or 'Miniatures', had the head and legs moulded as one with the body, only the arms were jointed. They had

Small Rosebud baby
for dressing

sleep eyes and a rather curious 'sucked cheeks' expression, but were very cute. In the 1960s, the faces were changed slightly to give the twins larger eyes and plumper cheeks. *Woman's Weekly* also provided patterns for the *Rosebud* Thumbsuck 6 inch babies.

   As mentioned in Chapter 2, *Woman* Magazine had a tie-in with the *Pedigree* Elizabeth doll, providing patterns for her designed by Veronica Scott. Many other magazines did similar things, supplying patterns for *Roddy*, *Palitoy* or *Tudor Rose* dolls. Sometimes knitting or sewing contests were organised, with prizes offered for the winner of the best doll's outfit.

   Many people remember their mothers, aunts or grannies making clothing for their dolls, such as Wendy Moorhen, who was born in 1947: 'So the 1950s are smack bang my childhood doll era.' Strangely, though, she can hardly remember anything about dolls to be played with, only her mother knitting the outfits: 'Mum was a great knitter and she had this wonderful pattern book with an entire ensemble, dress, jacket, coat, hat, bootees and, I am sure, several other items. The wool was a wonderful cherry red and some of the items were decorated with tiny white beads - I cannot believe mum sewed these on (sewing was my thing, crochet and knitting was hers) so I guess she enlisted my aunt's help. I can recall being so excited when I saw what she was doing and could hardly wait for each garment to be completed.' 50 years on, Wendy can't recall what became of the doll and outfit but she says that she has so much stuff in the loft, that she wonders if these items might just have

Doll submitted to a competition in the News Chronicle 1950s

survived in one of those many boxes she just refused to throw away when she married and left home. It would be wonderful if she could find these treasures – to discover a childhood doll which you thought you had lost is a very special feeling, a reminder of happy, carefree days.

Crafts

At the time, most girls owned sewing kits, while sets to embroider hankies or dressing table mats were popular gifts. Also popular were knitting sets with shorter, child-sized, colourful plastic knitting needles and balls of 'rainbow' wool – wool dyed in several colours to make knitting more interesting. Another girls' pastime was French knitting, which involved looping wool over one of four nails hammered into the top of a wooden cotton reel. A long tube of wool would slowly emerge through the hole in the reel, and could be coiled and sewn into place to form hats or mats.

Toy sewing machines were also in vogue; children were encouraged to use their hands. Although television sets were becoming more widespread in people's homes, children only watched for an hour or two (if they were lucky enough to be able to watch at all) so they needed hobbies.

Some companies produced kits of wool or fabric complete with a small doll. *Pedigree*, in conjunction with *Copley* knitting wools, issued a Little Gretel kit in the late 1950s which contained a pretty Delite girl, needles, pattern and some skeins of wool, to knit a 'playsuit' – stripy cardigan and trousers.

Also from *Pedigree* was a Little Mother Sewing/Knitting set containing a 6 inch Thumbsuck baby, a basket, fabric for lining the basket and wool, pattern and needles to knit a matinée set, and the *Pedigree* Twins – two small Thumbsucks in sleeping bags with wool, needles and pattern to make bonnets, booties and matinée jackets. Anne McAndrew learned to knit when she was eight, starting with an egg cosy, which made a good doll's hat. By 10 she had knitted a

Doll knitting patterns in *Woman's Weekly*

complete set of clothes for Sylvia, her *Pedigree* walker, which were displayed for parent's evening with lots of other knitting and sewing. Nowadays, sadly few primary schools would be able to mount a display of needle-work or knitting; these traditional skills are slowly being lost.

Knitting Patterns and Dress Patterns

Woman's magazines were inordinately popular in the 1950s – television still didn't have the grip it has today – and, for most married women, life revolved about the home. Magazines such as *Woman*, *Woman's Own*, *Woman's Weekly*, *People's Friend*, *My Weekly*, *Woman and Home* and *Woman's Realm* were lifelines, packed with household tips, short romantic stories, items about film stars: royalty, cookery recipes and, naturally, patterns for knitwear, needlework, dressmaking and embroidery. There was no Internet, of course, and many of today's distractions were unknown. Women didn't, in the main, socialise every evening; this was surprising given the relative freedom experienced by many women during the War when they took over the mens' jobs. They seemed quite content to return to being 'housewives'.

The magazine title most famed amongst today's collectors is *Woman's Weekly*. This magazine, which is still running, was first launched in 1911 and has a bias towards crafts, especially knitting and sewing. In the 1940s it introduced Twins, a pair of small *Rosebud* 7 inch high composition dolls, and the in-house designers produced many patterns for knitted outfits for the pair. There were cardigans, dresses and a school uniform. In the 1950s, the magazine switched to

Knitting pattern for doll's layette by Wolsey

hard plastic twins, and numerous patterns were printed in the magazine, which most weeks featured the twins on the cover. These *Rosebud* dolls had sucked in cheeks, sleep eyes and were jointed at the shoulders. Their wigs were mohair.

A couple of years later, *Woman's Weekly* introduced the small, $6^1/2$ inch Thumbsuck baby, again by *Rosebud*, so a layette could be knitted from patterns in the magazine (though the larger twins were still featured). A year later, Miss Rosebud came to the fore and *Woman's Weekly* stated, 'Our Twins are Growing Bigger.' Miss Rosebud is a particular favourite with today's collectors. (See Chapter 4). The magazine soon printed lots of patterns for this pretty $7^1/2$ inch doll, advertising her at 3/11d (20p). She was phased out in 1959, and the 1960s saw *Woman's Weekly* switch allegiance to the hard plastic *Chiltern* twins and also a pair of large vinyl Cheeky *Chiltern* dolls.

My Mum often knitted doll's clothes for me, using patterns gleaned from various magazines. One of my favourites was a pink dress to fit a 12 inch *Pedigree* girl; the lacy pattern of the skirt was knitted diagonally, which I always thought was such a clever thing to do. I still have that doll, Janice, and she still wears the dress. My aunt also used to sew doll's clothes for me. When I was small I took my composition baby to show a lady 'down the road' where we lived in Brixton. I have no idea of the lady's name but she knitted a beautiful green outfit for the doll; vest, knickers, dress, coat, bonnet, mittens and booties, edging the coat and hat with yellow fluffy wool. Doll lover Chris Garner, from Suffolk, relates that she was born in 1947 and has a younger sister and brother (born in 1952 and 1957 respectively.) She used to have pocket money at the rate of 1d per year; i.e. when she was nine she got 9d a week and so on. Chris remembers saving up her pocket money and buying a Miss Rosebud doll (4s 6d) and then making all her clothes. She says, 'Actually I don't think I had many bought clothes as things were not so easy as they are now and my mum and granny used to knit and sew!'

At first Chris used the patterns out of *Woman's Weekly* to make Miss Rosebud's clothes, but her local wool shop did not stock the 2-ply wool specified in the magazine and, as she had to resort to 3-ply, the clothes she knitted always turned out too big. She soon learnt though, and started making up her own patterns and if they turned out ok, wrote them down in a little notebook. It's a shame that she doesn't still have that notebook, as it would have been a fascinating 1950s memento!

Dolls' Clothes

Dolls' clothes in the 1950s tended to reflect the trends of the time, just as they do today. However, fashion, especially for children, was much more stable then, so most dressed dolls were sold in a sleeveless or short-sleeved frock made from cotton, seersucker, 'daphingle' (cotton with a raised pattern), taffeta, organdie, rayon or nylon, which was frequently flocked with a floral design. Many dresses had an attached apron, a reflection, perhaps, of the 1950s woman (who wore an apron for much of the day as she had so many chores). Bonnets were quite common, for both baby dolls and older girl dolls. Boy dolls wore short trousers and cotton tops, and babies wore one or two-piece romper suits. No stretchy all-in-one baby suits in those days! Knits were popular; many of these were created at home, see 'Knitting Patterns and Dress Patterns'.

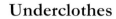

All-in-one undergarment for
Pretty Peepers by Pedigree

Underclothes

Underclothes were usually quite basic, as opposed to those worn by dolls in the early part of the century, and normally consisted of a pair of knickers in cotton, rayon or cotton jersey, frequently in a matching fabric to the dress. *Pedigree* were distinctive: many of their dolls, such as Little Princess, wore an all-in-one white, silky camisole/knickers type garment (often referred to as a 'onesie'). The *Pedigree* Pretty Peepers had the top of her camisole finished off with sleeves and collar to make a blouse, over which her pinafore was worn. *Rosebud*, too, often sold dolls in all-in-one camisoles, including a range intended for home dressing. Some of the composition singing dolls, by companies including *Mark Payne* and *Peter Darling*, wore ingenious knickers with a specially crafted slot at the front, through which the handle of the speech mechanism protruded.

Outfits

It is always a bonus to come across a 1950s doll wearing her original outfit, though it isn't always easy to recognise it as such. Certain companies, including *Pedigree*, were especially helpful, often labelling their dolls' clothes, whilst clothes made by the *Amanda Jane* (and the later, 1960s, *Faerie Glen*) Company also bore labels. In most cases, though, it's necessary to do a bit of detective work to try to determine the factory of

Undergarment on singing/speaking
composition doll, which allowed
mechanism to be operated through clothing

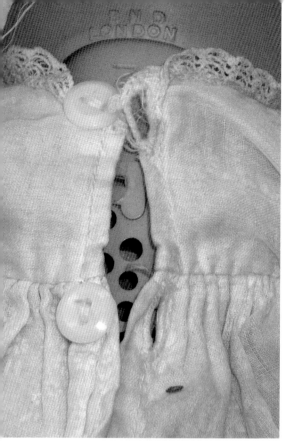

origin. Some clothes have distinctive fasteners, while others are of a recognisable style or are so obvious, they can't be anything else. For example, the wide collar dresses worn by *Pedigree's* Elizabeth: the girl-head patterned dress belonging to the *Palitoy* Girl doll or the matching needlecord dress and bonnets favoured by many of the *Linda* dolls.

Pedigree dresses had distinctive snap fasteners, with the top part in a ring so that the fabric showed through underneath, while *Palitoy* used small, coloured or white smooth snap fasteners. *Rosebud* dresses had small buttons with fasteners made from a twisted silky braid, rather than buttonholes. *BND*, who also used buttons, tended to use much larger buttons which often look out of proportion to the garment, or otherwise they used flat, matt buttons with two holes. The *Faerie Glen* dresses are easy to recognise, even if unlabelled, as the buttons fastened with shiny white plastic loops, while in the early 1950s, some companies, notably *Roddy* and *Tudor Rose*, used tiny gilt safety pins to fasten the doll's clothes, something which would never be allowed nowadays because of health and safety regulations.

Shoes

Dolls would also wear white silky knitted jersey socks and plastic shoes with round toes, which fastened by one plastic 'button' on the instep. Often, collectors refer to these shoes as 'Cinderella', as so many are marked this on the sole, and they were made by the London company, *Wilkinson and Gross*. The shoes came in many different sizes from tiny 05, to fit Miss Rosebud and similar dolls, up to size 7 which would suit a large walker with 5 inch long feet. There were other styles too, such as slip-ons, sandals and moccasins, all created from plastic.

Many companies, however, sold dolls wearing shoes marked with the company name, such as *Amanda Jane*, *Pedigree*, *BND* and *Roddy*. *Pedigree* dolls often wore a shoe which tied with silky laces, while some of the shoes worn by *Palitoy*, as well as those composition dolls still available, were made from a softer rubbery plastic. It was also quite fashionable to have a shoe moulded onto a dolls' foot, especially in the case of smaller dolls such as the Roddy Walkers. Very small dolls often had shoes painted direct onto their feet – sometimes the feet were moulded smoothly, without toes, but sometimes the foot was just painted black, even though the toes were there, giving a rather strange effect. Dolls with silver-painted shoes were normally fairies.

Wilkinson and Gross eventually transferred their business from London to Devon, and in the 1980s it was purchased by Frank and Anne Strudwick. They continued to produce Cinderella shoes, selling them through their shop, Children's Treasures, in Hastings. By the time the couple retired in 2001, production of the shoes had become uneconomical and the moulds were becoming worn, so they were all destroyed. This ended 50 years continuous production of the Cinderella shoes.

Cinderella shoes came in many styles

According to Frank, the *Wilkinson and Gross* company had also produced policemen's helmets for small costume dolls, and bagpipes for small Scottish dolls. They also made plastic bags, and, more importantly, the early hard plastic Jinx dolls (see Chapter 6), for the *Amanda Jane* company. Frank explains:

> *The smallest shoes marked Cinderella were the 05s. The largest were size 7. The styles that are marked Cinderella were the strap shoes, moccasins that tie with a ribbon, sandals, and Debutante shoes (slip-ons). In addition there were about four other slip-on styles that were unmarked but probably made by Wilkinson and Gross. These include high boots that we think were made for Sindy but can't be sure. When we bought the business from Derrirose we inherited a large stock of them. We also had a few very small unmarked slip-ons that may have been made for the small hard plastic costume dolls made in the 1950s.*

Today, collectors in Britain look out for Cinderella shoes to add a finishing touch to their 1950s doll collection. In America, similar styled shoes are known as 'Mary Janes'. Cinderella shoes came in many different colours, including white, black, brown, red, light blue, dark blue, pink, orange, turquoise, yellow, tan, green and lilac. The little 'button' fastening (a small plastic knob) had a tendency sometimes to ping out from the hole and get lost, but on the whole they were an ingenious little shoe.

Shoe Size Chart

Cinderella Shoe Measurements (in inches).
(Courtesy of Frank Strudwick.)

Size 05 (Smallest) 11 inches x 0.7 inches
Size 03 1.6 inches x 0.9 inches
Size 01 1.8 inches x 1.2 inches
Size 0 2.0 inches x 1.2 inches
Size 1 2.2 inches x 1.3 inches
Size 2 2.6 inches x 1.5 inches
Size 3 2.9 inches x 1.6 inches

Size 4 3.3 inches x 1.9 inches
Size 5 3.8 inches x 2.1 inches
Size 6 4.3 inches x 2.3 inches
Size 7 (Largest) 5.0 inches x 2.5 inches

All sizes are approximate. Although Sizes 02 and 04 were made in a different style of shoe it is not known whether strap shoes in these sizes were ever produced.

Accessories

Girls were still encouraged to be 'domesticated' and, for the majority of 1950s girls, university education was not an option. It was taken for granted that, on leaving school (at the age of 15 or 16) the average girl would get a job as a secretary, shop assistant or factory worker and soon find a husband. Then she would settle down to care for a home and raise their children. Once the children were of school age, then mothers might take a 'little part-time job'.

Therefore, for girls, toys of a domestic kind were very popular and, of course, provided enormous play value. Dolls' prams, cots, baths and highchairs were in great demand; girls often played with dolls until they reached their teens.

Prams and Pushchairs

Although we tend to think that after the war things soon returned to normal, they didn't, certainly not in the case of toys. The first few years were still affected by some toy shortages, not only caused by manufacturers having to get things organised and start producing once more, but because there was a huge baby boom after the war. Consequently, a whole new generation of children needed playthings, and often, there weren't enough to go round. I was lucky enough to have a small, red tin *Tri-ang* doll's pram in the late 1940s, but had outgrown it by 1951, and my mother had to search London, putting

Author and her beloved Dunkley pram, early 1950s

her name on lists and queuing, until she finally found a doll's pram for my fourth birthday. The pram she bought was made by *Dunkley*, who at the time were famed for both doll's prams and full-size versions.

Prams weren't the only product which *Dunkley* made; apparently they also made vehicles, including motorbikes. The company was established in 1874 as a perambulator manufacturer at Jamaica Row, Birmingham. In Victorian times it was necessary to be versatile and, according to a catalogue of 1880, they also made 'Prams, rocking horses, see-saws, pedal tricycles, hobby-horse tricycles, mail carts, steam circuses & roundabouts with organ complete'. Six years later they had the ingenious idea of making 'gas cars' which could be refilled by a rubber tube from gas street lamps. Later they moved into the field of motorbike manufacture, before amalgamating with the *Kensington Baby Carriage Company* and obtaining showrooms in London's West End. Their name became synonymous with prams up to the mid-1950s.

This is luxury

—comfort, style and safety
that delights the most exacting taste
The new Clarence by Pedigree

Pedigree
REGD TRADE MARK

Pedigree pram advert 1950s

My *Dunkley* doll's pram was pale dove grey with leather springs and a brake. It had a grey hood and matching storm apron, and the handle was made from a white ceramic-type material, with *Dunkley* emblazoned on it in script. Under the mattress was a 'secret compartment' to store doll's clothes and bedding. Later I was taken to a shop to buy a wicker pram basket which fitted on the back of the pram, to carry other treasures.

Though doll's prams were still hard to get during the first year or two of the 1950s, by the middle of the decade the choice was astounding; prams were not only made by toymakers such as *Tri-ang* (*Pedigree*), but by makers of full size prams including *Silver Cross*, *Marmet*, *Tan-Sad* and *Royale*. Prams were obtainable in all sizes, from small, lightweight metal varieties for toddlers to luxurious coach-built types for older girls, no different to those used by their mothers.

In the 1950s, Christine Garner had a doll's pram but doesn't know the make. It was a boxy shape made out of American cloth with an external metal frame. This pram was navy blue with a cream interior and had a working hood and apron and a foot operated brake. One day she decided it needed cleaning so took it indoors into the kitchen. Mum and Granny were occupied elsewhere in the house and Christine thought she would get on with her cleaning. What to use? Well, in those days her Mum had a box of Lux flakes (very expensive and only sparingly used for delicate woollens) which was kept with the other detergent powders (such as Oxydol and Tide). 'What a good idea to use the Lux flakes', Christine thought! She ran a bowl of warm water and tipped a good quantity, probably half the contents of the box, into her doll's pram. She was merrily scrubbing away when Mum and Granny, wondering what little Christine was doing as she was so quiet, came into the kitchen to investigate. As you can imagine, she was definitely not the 'flavour of the month' and got told off for not asking first, and also for using the Lux flakes. Christine was about five at the time.

Silver Cross was the most famous make of prams, and they are still made bearing this name, although the name has changed hands. The company began in 1877, when a gentleman called William Wilson started his own business manufacturing doll and baby carriages in Silver Cross Street, Hunslet. His first pram featured a unique suspension system and a reversible folding hood, both groundbreaking attributes at the time. In the 1920s, *Silver Cross*, by now a famed company, supplied a baby carriage to King George VI and Her Majesty Queen Elizabeth for their children, Princess Elizabeth and Princess Margaret Rose. Following this *Silver Cross* moved to larger premises at Guiseley.

During the war the company was requisitioned by the Air Ministry, and used to turn out 18 million parts for planes such as Spitfires and Hurricanes. After the war, many of the techniques were adapted and applied to the prams. Princess Elizabeth, later the Queen, chose a *Silver Cross* pram when Prince Charles was born in 1949. In the 1950s a series of iconic shaped prams were produced; the company was at the forefront of design.

1950s dolls' prams included; Susan, a deep metal twin pram which dipped in the middle, making it look rounded, mounted on leather straps: Greta, 'with enamelled wheels and levers and leathercloth hood and apron' which retailed at £10.15s: Valerie, a dipping, rounder-bodied pram with chromed or colour-enamelled wheels: Vicky boasting 'chromium wheels and levers' retailing at £13. 10s, and the classic Rose, which featured a Wedgwood plaque with a rose design on either side of the chassis. *Silver Cross* prams are still made today with plaques, including a Beatrix Potter or Winnie the Pooh range, as well as a rose.

Margaret Follwell, an avid collector from Wiltshire, explained how, in June 1950, she was taken to London and was bought a *Silver Cross* doll's pram – and she wishes she still had it! It had a coffee body and a darker coffee hood and apron. There was also a wicker pram basket and her grandfather also bought her a Moreland Dolls Sun Canopy – it was cream with a dark green lining and a long cream fringe. On the way home from London they had to go in the mail carriage with the glorious pram. As Margaret's brother, who was only two, was very sleepy, Margaret's mother put him in the pram all the way home. Many 1950s prams were so sturdy and well sprung that small tots could sleep in them quite happily. My *Dunkley* often had a 'real baby' sleeping in it, when friends of my parents came to visit.

Another well known make at the time was *Mobo*. *Mobo* toys were made by *D. Sebel and Co.*, in Erith, Kent, and the company was set up in 1947. *Mobo* were especially famed for their various large metal toys, such as colourful ride-on horses, sit upon giant metal snails, a

Tin pram by Mobo

'toy-toise' and a range of sturdy scooters. My scooter was a *Mobo*, with a brake, and my Mum and Dad bought it for me when I was four or five, as an unbirthday present. We had gone to a toyshop, I can't recall where, but it might have been in Camberwell, London. Dad must have had a bit of extra money that week, as normally cash was tight; I remember that the lady in the shop asked if it was my birthday and when I said no, told me I was a very lucky girl.

Mobo also made desks, pedal cars, trikes, wheelbarrows, and of course, dolls's prams. One often found today is a pram intended for the smaller child, and painted a pretty shade of sky blue. Clearly marked *Mobo*, this particular model was called Diana, and has a handle height of 20 inches. It is 13 inches high and 17 inches long, perfect for a toddler. Also advertised in the *Mobo* catalogue is a 'magic pushchair', a very sturdy-looking contraption, which boasts 'Touch the handle and surprise, dolly moves and dolly cries'!

Tan-Sad's 1950s doll's prams included Vera, a collapsible 23 inch long, rather boxy looking little pram, made from leathercloth. It was available in assorted colours, amongst them royal blue, beige or grey, and advertised as folding 'easily and compactly.' Another model, the Dolls Cot Kar was a coach-built pram with a drop foot, braided, leather cloth hood, and came in the same colours as the previous model. According to the blurb, 'You meet the best little people in Tan-Sad toys'! The company, from Birmingham, also made scooters, trikes, pedal cars and a 'play car', which resembled a small seat with a tray on wheels.

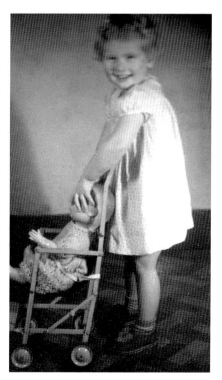

Author and pushchair

Pushchairs would either be lightweight foldaway types, often with metal frames and canvas or oilcloth seats, or quite heavy, solid all-metal pushchairs, sturdy enough to take a small toddler. There were in those days, of course, no lightweight aluminium-framed buggies. *Tri-ang* was a particularly popular maker of doll's pushchairs during the 1950s, and these are still easy to find today. I had a *Tri-ang* doll's pushchair, with a blue flat metal frame and a black oilcloth seat. This was a lightweight version, and the seat was unsupported, just suspended from a strut at the top and wrapped around a wooden roller at the bottom. There was a strap to keep my doll firmly in place.

Currys had a special Christmas offer in the mid 1950s – you could buy a 20 inch long *Tri-ang* doll's pram, complete with an undressed 16 inch *Pedigree* Delite baby doll, and a free P&B knitting patterns book for 62/8 (£3.14p), postage 2/5 (12p). The advert said the offer was obtainable, 'From your local branch of Currys or posted to your favourite niece anywhere in U.K.', adding, 'Special greetings card enclosed.' What a wonderful present that would have been to a little girl from a kind uncle.

Anne McAndrew had a *Silver Cross* dolls pushchair and one notable week, when she was five, her grandmother pushed her in it to the doctor's and back, two miles away. Poor Anne had to have an injection each day, and was too sore to walk. Her gran was not a well lady either, though luckily short, so didn't have to stoop to reach the handle, otherwise she does not know how she would have managed. There was not a bus route in that direction and one didn't use a taxi in those days; indeed there was no way of contacting one, as Anne's family, like most people at that time, didn't have a telephone. This just shows how sturdy the *Silver Cross* doll's pushchairs were – capable of taking the

Small Tudor Rose doll's highchair

weight of a five year old for a four mile trip. No wonder so many pushchairs and prams from the era have survived.

Highchairs

Highchairs were usually of wood, either painted or natural, and many of them featured a folding mechanism which converted the highchair into a low chair and feeding table at the press of a lever or two. Highchairs normally had a row of plastic beads along the tray, and the tray would lift up, just like a full size one, to allow the doll to fit inside. They usually had a foot rest too, though unless the child was fortunate enough to own a large knee bend doll, it was unlikely that the dolls feet would ever make contact with it. Sometimes the chairs had small wooden wheels, so that they could convert into wheeled carts.

Cots and Cradles

Dropside cots, carry cots and cradles were all popular in the 1950s. Particularly in vogue were folding metal framed cradles which were draped with fine printed cotton coverings, usually a dainty floral. A metal bar with a right-angle bend slotted vertically into one end, to support a matching cotton, frilled hood. The whole thing was supported on the metal frame by hooks so it could be rocked. I loved my blue draped cot, it was like a bed for a princess, and my favourite doll always slept there.

Carry cots were often quite large and, though could be collapsed down, were usually left up and made rigid with the use of thin plywood boards, which fitted into the base, sides and ends under the plastic covering. A curved soft hood and matching apron completed the cot. The cot structure was normally a pastel leather-look soft plastic. My pink carry cot was one of my special toys, because I thought it was such a 'grown-up' thing to own, like a real baby's cot.

I was overjoyed when I finally found it again, about 10 years ago, at my aunt's home. It was now missing the hood and cover, but at least I have my cot back! Christine Garner says that her sister had a doll's cot which was constructed in a similar fashion to her dolls pram, with a metal frame painted blue, but she doesn't know the maker. It had a cloth body interior suspended from the frame, with a frill all round of gauzy material. A metal support at the back held up a canopy of the same stuff and the whole thing was trimmed with a lacy edging.

Baths and Bath Sets

Bath sets were particularly popular, and most manufacturers seemed to produce them. Normally they consisted of a plastic bath, a small doll, a towel, a flannel and a bar of soap. Companies such as *Pedigree*, *Tudor Rose*, *Rosebud* and *Bluebox* issued these sets, as well as selling baths separately. Pretty *Rosebud* sets advertised in 1957 included not only a vinyl doll, soap, sponge, flannel, towel and bowl, but a set of clothes and a 'packet of real soap powder' called Clozone. The sets cost 12/6d (63p) each, wholesale.

Tudor Rose bath set

Other Accessories

Toy washing machines, irons, ironing boards, mangles, brooms, dustpans and brushes, vacuum cleaners, carpet sweepers, laundry sets, pastry sets and cooking stoves could also be seen in all the toyshops, while a huge array of dolls crockery and cutlery was available. Pastry sets in particular were deemed useful gifts and, as

Doll's laundry set

most children wanted to be 'like Mummy', were much liked. They normally included a wooden rolling pin, selection of metal (sometimes plastic) pastry cutters and a metal patty pan or two (these pans were usually of very thin tin and unsuitable for a real oven). Anne McAndrew recalls having a tin oven and a lovely set of cooking utensils. She was allowed to bake tiny buns in the bun tin, and used the rolling pin on cut off bits of pastry. I, too, used to have 'baking days' armed with my little wooden rolling pin. My Mum taught me to make jam tarts, rolling the pastry out time and again (I fear it must have gone very grey!) before cutting little shapes with a pastry cutter, and filling them with jam.

Products such as 'My Doll's Laundry Set' by *Mayfair*, which consisted of a doll-size apron, clothes pegs, clothes line, coat hanger and a cake of soap or cleaning sets (containing brushes, dusters, carpet beaters, cloths and a feather duster) were loved by small girls.

Christine Garner remembers that she used to have dollies' washing days, collecting up all her dolls' clothes and giving them a good wash. Her mum has a photo somewhere of Christine helping to hang out the washing, including the dolls' clothes – it was a lovely sunny morning in the garden and she must have been about eight. This triggered many memories for me – I can recall washing my

Doll's cutlery set

doll's clothes, the suds running along my arms and dripping on the floor. Each dress was scrubbed on a corrugated glass washboard. I had a small toy mangle, and used to put each little garment through to squeeze out the water.

Doll's crockery, especially, is in demand with collectors nowadays, particularly character types featuring Mickey Mouse, Little Noddy, Sooty, Muffin the Mule or other 1950s favourites. Some sets were made from china, but many were made from tin, aluminium or plastic, and doll tea parties were very popular amongst children. It was the norm for children to invite friends 'to tea', where they would eat sandwiches, small cakes and scones and drink tea or milk. Now, that meal has largely disappeared except for special occasions.

Tea sets were usually sold packed in prettily-printed cardboard boxes, with the set being nicely displayed when the lid was opened; each plate, cup and saucer neatly slotting into its allotted place with the all-important tea pot taking pride of place. A 1957 *Ellar* catalogue, containing various items, was selling a doll's pottery nursery-rhyme design 2 cup tea set for 11/- (60p) each (wholesale), while 2 cup plastic sets were 69/- (£3.45p) a dozen (wholesale). *Ellar* was a trademark of *Leon Rees and Co.*, who were owners of *Chiltern* toys, and also distributors for other companies.

One particularly attractive doll's tea set was made from creamy-white china, and commemorated the 1953 Coronation of Queen Elizabeth. It was marked 'Corona' and made by *Royal Cauldon*. Beautifully decorated,

Doll's Coronation tea-set

it featured the head of the new Queen, as well as designs of flags, insignias and inscriptions. Sets such as this are sought after today, not just by doll collectors, but also by collectors of commemorative china. Commemorative pieces have the advantage that, being dated pieces, there can be no doubt as to when they were made.

Tea sets gave enormous play value; every one liked to give tea parties. Anne McAndrew went one better with the games she played with her grandmother. She says, 'Nanna and I would play Lyons Cafés. We would get out my pink plastic tea set. We had iced gems and real tea in my teapot. I had to go round the table with a tray collecting all I wanted and pay my money. I had a little till.' I can remember those tills, we called them 'cash registers', and I had one as well. Mine had sturdy plastic keys and when you pressed them, they went 'ting' and a price popped up in the plastic window, such as 1d or 1/-. I used to play shops with mine, using packets and boxes from Mum's larder.

Doll's Houses and Other Toys

I can't remember when I was given my doll's house, but imagine it was around 1950, when I was three. The house was made by *Tri-ang*, a basic, four roomed box type. The house itself was wood, with cardboard floors printed with shiny paper carpets. The front of the house was made of a cream tin, and was hinged. There were pink roses painted onto the front, and there was a sundial above the red metal door. Either side of the front door were two 'real' fir trees in pots, which fixed into holes by the doorstep, and the house

**Basic Tri-ang No 50
doll's house**

featured two bay windows. Recently I discovered that the houses bearing the rose design were amongst the first produced after the war, and the roses were painted by hand. Apparently, my house was a *Tri-ang* No. 50, and was made at the factory in Merthyr Tydfil. Later, the design was replaced by one of yellow laburnum plants, and the houses bearing these are much easier to find nowadays.

Inside my doll's house was a mixture of furniture, much of it made by *Kleeware*. It had a white fridge, kitchen table, chairs and sink. There were tiny metal cooking utensils such as saucepans and frying pans. The lounge had brown furniture with cream legs and, one of my favourite pieces, a standard lamp with a pleated plastic shade. Another favourite piece, also in the lounge, was a black grand piano. Later, my Dad made me a staircase for the house and cut a hole in the dividing panel for access – I couldn't have my little dolls climbing the stairs and being unable to enter the rooms upstairs when they arrived!

The house was populated with a selection of small plastic and soft rubber dolls, many, again, by *Kleeware*. I adored my tiny doll's pram, which must have been about 3 inches long. It was of cream metal and bore a picture on the side of a lady pushing a pram. And on that picture of a pram, was a picture of the lady pushing a pram – for the first time I was suddenly struck with the concept of infinity. I often used Dobbin, a grey metal cart horse from my farm, to pull a little cart which my Dad had made me, and which carried the occupants of the doll's house. The cart, I remember, was made from sturdy card with hardboard wheels.

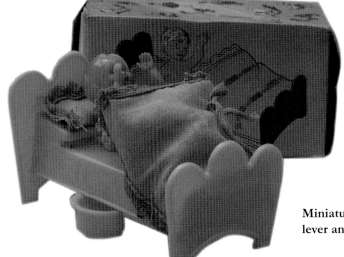

Anne McAndrew's dolls house had been made by her Dad out of a packing case, with *Kleeware* dolls furniture. She had a green *Minic* clockwork car that she kept with the dolls house, and she used to

Miniature doll in bed – move lever and doll sits on potty!

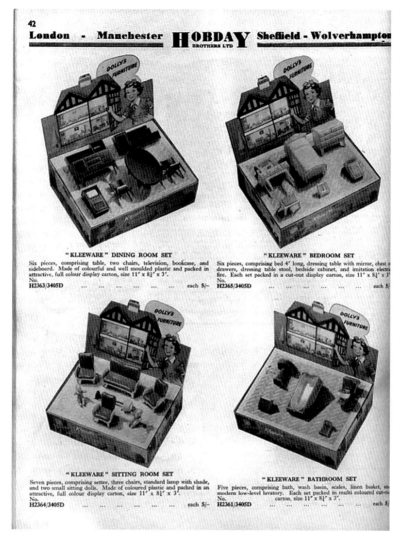

Advertisement for Kleeware doll's house furniture

put the room light out and put a torch in the house so it appeared as if the lights were on. She had a little room upstairs next to her bedroom, from 1956, which became her toy room in the summer time. There was no heating upstairs and this room had no light. Anne used to play schools with her toys; she had a *Tri-ang* desk and chair, and a board and easel. She used to give all the toys pieces of paper to do their sums on. Apart from Sylvia, her 22 inch *Pedigree* walker and her 16 inch bent leg hard plastic baby, there were two material dolls.

Rosebud boy at school!

She also had a nurse, an 8 inch *Tudor Rose* black HP, and both black and white *Roddy* 10 inch babies. There was also a Teddy Bear. Even the elephant doorstop sometimes went to school! Another of Anne's memories is of receiving a *Mobo* scooter when she was seven; it had a brake, which was very useful as she lived at the top of a hill!

It seems that 1950s children all tended to own similar toys – we all had *Mobo* scoters, *Tri-ang* desks and chairs, *Kleeware* doll's house furniture and little wooden rolling pins. However, my dolls were always my favourite toys and once we had moved from Brixton, to a house in Welwyn Garden City where I had a bedroom of my own, I would spend many happy hours playing dolls and doll's tea-parties. I had a collection of doll's clothes, and I used to sometimes make doll's dresses from odd scraps of fabric and ribbon, but, unlike many others of my generation, never made complete outfits – my knitting was never more adventurous than doll's scarves! Christine Garner was creative, remembering, 'We had a lovely time with our dolls and gave them all names. They were educated in our dollies' school. We also ran a dolls' library and they occasionally had their hair done at our dolls' hairdressers.' I just hope the trips to the hairdressers didn't involve cutting of the hair! The trouble with many of the 1950s dolls was that (because the wigs were glued-on mohair), shampooing would cause the hair to fall off, as would vigorous brushing and combing. Once the rooted vinyl heads were introduced, in the late 1950s, no doubt Mums heaved sighs of relief, knowing that they would no longer need to keep taking their daughter's dolls to the doll hospital for a new wig.

Packaging

Some of the most attractive packaging emanates from the 1950s; boxes, brochures and packet tops used artists' depictions rather than photographs. The majority of work is very much a wishful kind of thinking, with dolls running, dancing, kneeling and wearing beautiful full-skirted dresses. Children's hopes must have often been raised on receiving such a box, then cruelly dashed when the doll inside was plain, unjointed and wearing a short wisp of cotton.

However, from a collector's point of view, these retro boxes are delightful, and frequently refer to the Little Mother, Mummy's Helper or Dolly's Own; names which would be treated scornfully today. Some dolls came in plain cardboard boxes, often bearing hand-written labels stating the colour of the doll's hair, dress or size, but many 1950s boxes were decorated prettily with nursery characters or animals, or a drawing depicting the doll. The benefit of these boxes meant that a doll could be stored safely, which is why so many dolls from the era are being found today in excellent condition: the use of eye-catching designs made closed boxes just as tempting to prospective customers. Although a drawback was that the dolls couldn't easily be seen when in the shops, many shopkeepers displayed the dolls with the box tops removed. However, a vast quantity of dolls, especially those sold in Woolworths and other chain stores, had no boxes and were displayed on the open counters. This made doll buying a long task, as every doll looked slightly different and needed to be studied with care!

Beautiful packaging
on a Pedigree Little
Princess box

Some boxes were stunning, such as the design on the box for the
Pedigree Little Princess (See Chapter 2). This box featured a depiction of
Buckingham Palace, with the doll standing in front. Often, though, the
artwork enhanced a doll, making for a item so pretty that the box was
saved, even by children who would normally discard it without a second
thought – a bonus for the collector who happens upon one later. It's a
really lucky find when leaflets, hang tags and brochures are also found
with the box.

Chapter 9

Celebrations

Wearing the traditional rose-coloured spectacles and looking back to the 1950s, as a child it seemed that Easter was always sunny, summer was always long, warm and rain-free, while Christmas was always snowy. I'm sure there were rainy Easters, cold summers and snowless Christmases, but those have been obliterated from my memory.

Dolls were given for birthdays and Christmases, normally. If a child had been ill, or good, or saved up her pocket money, then she might get another doll, but in general girls didn't own even a fraction of the toys a child owns today. They were very popular as birthday presents. I recall a friend being given a large yes/no doll. This doll shook or nodded her head at the push of a button. She wanted me to ask a question of the doll, but I could only come out with the most inane 'Do you like salad?', (something I loathed at the time). Everyone seemed to think it funny, and the doll nodded enthusiastically to show that, yes, she did indeed like salad very much.

Doll collector Anne McAndrew of Essex says that she remembers going to Cowells toy shop in Ipswich. There she saw lots of lovely toys and in particular dolls. When asked which she liked she pointed to a *Pedigree* 22 inch walker with auburn hair and a green striped dress. On her fifth birthday she was given an enormous box and when she opened the lid there was the doll, Sylvia. Anne can still remember how excited she was. She had a birthday party that afternoon with some other little girls from her road. She remembered they played hide and seek, 'what's the time Mr. Wolf' and pass the parcel, but Anne just wanted to play with her doll. This was 1953 and Sylvia was the last doll Anne had as a present. Her friend from up the road had a *Pedigree* walker as well, so they played with them together a lot. These *Pedigree* 22 inch walkers were incredibly popular, and obviously made to last, which is why they are so easy to find today.

Christmas

Christmas was the time of dolls. It was, especially, the time when small dolls came into their own, dolls just the right size for perching on top of the Christmas tree. In the 1950s, everyone had a fairy on the tree, it was tradition. No one had stars or angels. At least no one I knew. And of course, Christmas was a red, green and white time, just as Easter was blue, green and yellow – I always used to think of events in colour.

Christmas Dolls

All girls at the time seemed to want a new doll for Christmas; girls played with dolls right up till they began senior school (and sometimes after!) Toy shops and department stores were crammed with dolls in the 1950s, even shops such as Marks and Spencer and British Home Stores. The dolls were made by many different companies, so all looked different (unlike today, when toy companies tend to come under one or two umbrellas, so the majority of dolls look the same). The range of sizes was vast, from $1/2$ inch high rubber doll's house dolls to 36 inch high

Roddy Fairy

walkers. Christmas afternoon was spent taking your new doll for a stroll in your doll's pram, inevitably meeting friends who were doing the same thing.

Pauline Payne from Norwich says that she was born in 1946 and for the Christmas of 1957 wanted a walker doll, but her mother said she was much too old to have any more dolls. However, on Christmas morning at the bottom of her bed, there was a lovely *Pedigree* flirty eye walker doll. Her mother had dressed her in a blue seersucker dress, and a very pretty bonnet. Pauline still has that doll and the earlier two; a 'Made in England' baby doll dressed by her grandmother in a knitted layette, and an HP doll which was also a walkie/talkie.

My clearest Christmas memory was of finding a *Pedigree* Beauty Skin in a pretty draped crib when I was five. (See Chapter 6.) I also recall getting a toy consisting of a plastic roundabout topped with Dutch boy and girl rubber dolls, and a baby tied to a cord. When the baby was placed at the edge of a table, he unwound, causing the roundabout to spin and making it seem as though the two Dutch dolls were looking for him. This toy made a great impact on me, partly because I remember it hanging from Dad's arms when he and Mum crept up to my bed on Christmas Eve with my presents.

I remember, too, Mum's panic-stricken whisper of, 'She's still awake' and I jammed my eyes tight shut – and must have instantly dropped off to sleep, because when I awoke it was morning and the Dutch roundabout toy was by my bed. I would have been three or four, and I think that was the Christmas I started to wonder about the existence of Father Christmas! The other reason it made an impact

Tudor Rose Fairy

was the smell – the rubber had a strong, though not-unpleasant smell. I still have the Dutch boy, and I only have to open his box to breathe in the smell and have that Christmas come racing back.

Margaret Follwell wanted a walkie talkie doll, with blonde hair, blue eyes and a hat and coat with fur on it. On Christmas morning she was so excited with her new acquisition, who she named Sylvia, that Margaret took her round to see her next door neighbour who was an elderly lady. Of course she had to walk her. When they got to her back door the neighbour was standing there waiting – but disaster – when Margaret picked Sylvia up her leg fell off. You can imagine how upset Margaret was. Her father rushed to see what was the matter and of course said, 'I told you not to walk her on the rough concrete ground, but never mind, I'll fix her up as good as new'. Margaret believed her Dad could do anything, and proclaims, 'Well, he did mend her leg by making a metal plate … she was my pride and joy.'

Fairies

Sometimes the fairy would be an heirloom doll, one which was unwrapped from her tissue every year, placed reverently atop the tree to cast her Christmas spells, then squirreled away on twelfth night to sleep for another year. It's still possible to find these treasured dolls today, amazingly pristine, with their cardboard wings still intact, their tissue petticoats crisp, and their white net dresses, though maybe a little dingy, still sometimes bearing the faint scent of pine needles from Christmases past. Although their tinsel might be tarnished with age, this just adds to their charm. It's a special find when you come across one of these still-perfect dolls, because it enables you to carry on the doll's tradition, allowing her to preside over the festivities once more, even though she may now be adorning a plastic, rather than a real, tree. As you fasten her in place, you can't help but wonder what sights she has seen over her 50 or so Christmases.

Many families, such as mine, however, popped along to Woolworths each December and bought a plastic fairy dressed in

crepe paper with tinsel wings. When the festivities were over, the doll was given to the daughter to play with and I well recall the excitement of being handed a Christmas fairy - she was always the most special doll of all. All too soon, of course, the crepe paper had split and the fairy's wings had fallen off. Then she reverted to being another plastic doll, ready to be dressed in a knitted outfit or scrap of cotton fabric, which explains why nowadays small plastic 1950s dolls are found sporting silver painted feet, but wearing everyday clothes!

To many people, the epitome of the English fairy doll is the hard-plastic type, dressed in paper, net, muslin or rayon, lavishly decorated with glitter and tinsel, with a wand made from a glittery star mounted on a

Unmarked fairy dressed in crepe paper – 'Now you see her – Now you don't!'

thin wire rod pushed through a hole in her hand. Often the wings were made from silver card or fine gauze sprinkled with glitter, and dolls such as these were made by most manufactures famed for their plastic dolls, including *Airfix*, *Pedigree*, *Tudor Rose*, *Rosebud*, *Roddy*, *Palitoy* and *Sarold*. A more unusual kind, which surfaced for a couple of years in the early 1950s, was a tiny plastic doll dressed in shiny card with a matching pointed hat in the style of a Medieval lady and swirly wings. These came in assorted colours, and I can remember being entranced by one which my mother bought, dressed in cerise-pink shiny card. I'd never seen a bright pink fairy before.

Interestingly, it appears that there was a company specialising in fairy wands, which sold them to the various doll manufacturers, because so many fairy dolls dating from the late 1940s, as well as the 1950s and 1960s, bore identical wands, even though the dolls originated from different factories. These wands consisted of a metal rod, around 3-4 inches long, with a sturdy cardboard star fixed to the top. This star would be thickly coated with glitter, which, over the years, tended to grow dull and tarnished.

Airfix Fairies

Fairy dolls which were particularly popular at the time were those made by the *Airfix* company. More known today for their plastic kits, these small dolls were tiny, just 4 inches high, and were dressed as fairies in crepe paper skirts which were sometimes topped with net or gauze. Naturally the skirts soon tore and split so if you can find one in perfect condition, it's a bonus. These fairies carry wands topped with a glitter-sprinkled cardboard star (though the later models have plastic stars) and their moulded hair is topped with a tinsel crown. Just like many other fairy dolls of the 1950s, these were sold very cheaply in stores such as Woolworths. There was also a range of small unmarked fairies with attached gold plastic wings and gold-painted hair moulded into a short, wavy bob, which are becoming quite collectable today.

Airfix fairy

Roddy Palmolive promotional fairy

Roddy Fairies

The Palmolive soap company ran a promotion for a fairy doll in 1957. The fairy would be sent out in return for a small sum of money and some wrappers from soap bars. Customers were sent a small blonde fairy doll made by *Roddy*, dressed in white satin edged with silver braid and carrying a wand. Because they came handily packaged in a cardboard box, many people prudently repacked the dolls after use, and so there are quite a few of these dolls in good condition still around. If you are very lucky, they might even have the accompanying, very polite, letter from the Colgate-Palmolive company which stated:

> *I am sorry that I have been compelled to send you a circular letter, but so great has been the demand for our little Palmolive Fairy Doll that it has been impossible to write to everyone individually.*
>
> *Owing to the demand, which is exceeding all expectations, a slight delay in mailing may occur in some cases, for which we are sorry, However, at very short notice, more Fairy Dolls are being specifically made by our suppliers and we can guarantee all requests being met… but the offer must definitely close on January 31st 1958.*
>
> *If, therefore, you know any friends who would like a Fairy doll, please be sure to tell them to write in very soon to avoid disappointment. The address is on this letter, but envelopes should clearly be marked 'Department R.'*

This letter reflects a difference of attitudes to today's promotional offers - now, you are lucky if you even get a compliments slip.

Though these are *Roddy* dolls, they bear more than a passing resemblance to the small hard plastic dolls made by *Chiltern*.

Rosebud Fairies

Some of the prettiest fairies were those made from the Miss Rosebud dolls – as these dolls were beautiful whatever they wore, sparkly fairy dresses made them stunning. At 8 inches high, they looked perfect in their sequin-scattered net skirts: silver-ribbon bodices and wings made from fine gauze. Miss Rosebuds were jointed dolls with sleep eyes, soft mohair wigs and flushed faces. More commonly found, however, are the 7 inch *Rosebud* girls with unjointed straight legs, moveable arms, sleep eyes and glued-on mohair wigs. Sometimes, these dolls bore a sucked in expression, though most are charming. *Rosebud* also sold some of their little dolls as cheeky Pixies, festively dressed in red and green, with pointed ear flaps on their hats.

Rosebud Christmas pixies

Other Fairies

Plenty of today's collectors seek out the adorable chubby-cheeked *Roddy* 'thumbs-up' fairy dolls, with sleep eyes, smiling mouths and thumbs pointing skywards – although hands like those must make it rather difficult for a fairy to grip her wand! Other little fairy dolls which a collector might come across include *Pedigree* Delites with their 'starfish hands' – fingers spread wide – and *Tudor Rose*, which were enormously popular dolls at the time as they were sold cheaply in toy shops. These had sweet, solemn faces which lent themselves well to a watchful fairy. Often, small dolls such as this were dressed at home. Home-dressed fairies are a very important part of our history, and should be regarded as 'original', even though they are not 'factory dressed.'

Doris Howe from Suffolk remembers, 'My first job in 1952 was in weaving and spinning. I was paid £1.00 a week. My first ever doll in a box was a nude *Rosebud* which cost me an eighth of my wages, 2 shillings and sixpence, now equal to $12^1/2$ p. I dressed her for our Christmas tree which is where she has spent every Christmas since, first in my family home, then in my own home. She has been redressed quite a few times over the years!

Author and her rubber Baby David doll on beach 1950s

Summer Holidays

Apart from Christmas and Easter, the other major event in a child's calendar was the annual summer holiday. Going abroad wasn't an option in the 1950s, you had to be really rich to do that. Holidays in the early 1950s involved carrying heavy attaché cases onto a train, or, more often, a coach, to be magically transported to Clacton, Brighton, Southend, Blackpool or Skegness, depending on where you lived. We stayed in a caravan, sharing washing facilities and toilets

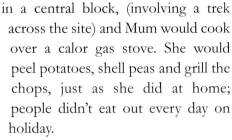

in a central block, (involving a trek across the site) and Mum would cook over a calor gas stove. She would peel potatoes, shell peas and grill the chops, just as she did at home; people didn't eat out every day on holiday.

Naturally, I used to take my dolls with me. One year I was allowed to take my folding carrycot, too, packed at the bottom of my parent's big suitcase. My dolls used to come to the beach with me, especially a rubber baby which I had called Baby David. I have no idea what make he was, but I do remember that the rubber peeled over time and he took on a jaundiced tone. Mum repainted the yellowy bits so, for a while at least, he would be pink again. I loved Baby David very much, and spent happy hours rolling him in the sand and then dunking him in my tin bucket.

Pedigree Delite ready for the beach

Anne McAndrew's first doll memory is when 'My Dad and Nanna took me to Potter Higham. We stayed for a week in a bungalow by the Broads. Dad fished most of the time. One day I remember him rowing me to the stores. I was about three or four and very shy. The lady in the shop took down a doll from the top shelf and gave it to me. She said it was the end of the season. It was unclothed and was a 16 inch bent leg HP. It was unmarked, I think a *Pedigree* and I have never found an exact replica. My Nanna had been a lady's maid when young, and made beautiful clothes for her young lady, so she soon made Dolly Daydream a dress and knitted her some clothes from the *Woman's Weekly* magazines. This doll went everywhere with me, and I have a few hazy photographs of her.'

Apart from Christmas, the only dolls I recall associated with special events were those produced for the Coronation – though one year my mother did dress up one of my baby dolls as a Happy New Year baby. The 1950s really was a doll-lover's paradise – if you had the money. Unlike today, dolls were expensive compared to the weekly wage, which is why the smaller dolls were so popular. At the dawn of the decade the average annual income was £101, yet, as an example, a 14 inch *Pedigree* girl doll cost just over £1 (which is why many children had to settle for smaller, unbranded dolls). Many major factories sold unbranded ranges of their dolls through chain stores, often undressed and normally just marked 'Made in England'. These can often be recognised by examining marked examples of similar dolls.

Yet, as we played with our dolls we could never possibly have dreamt that 50 years later those same dolls could be really valuable commodities. And manufacturers would no doubt have been horrified to learn that their new wonder product, plastic, did have a fault after all – years later, the spectre of 'hard plastic disease' reared its head. Luckily, the majority of doll collectors will never encounter it, although it is something which needs to be kept in mind.

Chapter 10

Repairing 1950s Dolls

Dolls from the 1950s will have celebrated their own 50th birthdays, so must be excused if they look rather worse for wear. Of course, if you are very fortunate, the doll you find will be mint, perfect, well-cared for and maybe still boxed. However, the majority of these dolls will have been played with and loved – so what can you do to freshen then up?

As long as a little common sense is used – no abrasives or harsh chemicals for instance – there is no reason why hard plastic dolls can't be made to look, if not as good as new, certainly good enough to display. All you need is a little time and a bit of effort. The first thing to remember is that, unlike modern dolls, hard plastic dolls

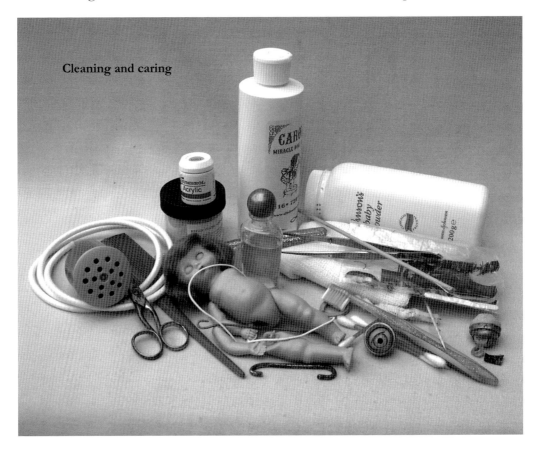

Cleaning and caring

should not be immersed in water. I know that at the time children did play with dolls in the bath and even in the sea (I used to!) but it certainly isn't good to get water entering the eyes or through the limb sockets. Limbs are often attached with metal hooks, while eyes sometimes have metal sockets; these will rust if soaked and can cause all kinds of problems.

Cleaning

If your hard plastic doll is grimy, the best way to remove the dirt is by using the softly, softly approach. You will need some soap – preferably a pure soap such as that sold for babies, with no additives or perfume which could be detrimental to the plastic. Then find two white cloths, maybe muslin or towelling, and a couple of white towels. (Coloured towels may be fine, but just occasionally a plastic doll can pick up dye from towelling and so it is best not to take the risk.)

Fill two small bowls with warm water, putting one aside for rinsing (I find small pudding basins are perfect). Moisten one of the white cloths, wrap it around your index finger and briefly rub it onto the bar of soap (just enough to impart a light film of soap on the cloth). Lay the doll onto one of the white towels, then carefully clean her face, taking care to avoid the eyes. Be careful with the lips and cheeks too, as some dolls can shed their colour when they get wet. Working one small section at a time use the spare white cloth, and the bowl of water which you put aside, to rinse each section as you go – but only make the cloth damp, don't soak it. You can wash the whole doll in this way. Make sure that water doesn't drip into the vent holes on the mama unit when you reach that area. You should find that the doll is already looking much happier!

Use a damp cotton bud to clean the ears and also between fingers and toes if necessary. You can also, very lightly, use a damp bud on the eyes, but be careful not to push too hard, and don't allow any water to seep into the sockets. You may find that you have to repeat the whole of the cleaning process at least once more, as it is very easy to miss a bit. It helps if you work at a table in natural light, maybe near a window, or even in the garden.

Makeup

Children enjoyed 'decorating' dolls. This can sometimes cause problems. Most common is nail varnish on toes and fingers. This can be removed using a non-acetone nail varnish remover, but it is very important to get the remover only on the varnish and not on the rest of the finger. Apply with a cotton bud or fine paintbrush. Lipstick can sometimes be removed by gently scraping any thick residue with a skewer or cocktail stick, then trying a grease-shifting product such as makeup remover, mild washing up liquid or a mild liquid (non abrasive) kitchen cleanser. 1950s lipsticks (and eyeshadows) often relied on stronger dyes than their modern counterparts and this can cause problems – however, unlike vinyl, makeup and other products tend to lie on top of the plastic rather than soak in, so normally cleaning with mild soap, as described above, is sufficient.

Cigarette Smoke

Cigarette smoke can cause tremendous harm to dolls; it is one of their worst enemies. Over the years, exposure to the smoke and nicotine can badly stain a doll, turning the plastic, hair and clothing a uniform shade of brown. It also makes them smell badly, and this smell can be very difficult to remove, especially from mohair wigs.

The cleaning process with mild soap will normally freshen up a smoke-caked doll, and it can be eye-opening to see the brown grime collected by the cloth. However, the hair can prove a problem as mohair isn't the easiest product to wash. (See Wigs.) The best cure for the smell is to wait for mild, slightly breezy days and leave the doll outside in a shady place. You will probably need to repeat this several times. The clothing should be laundered, and will probably need

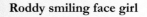

Roddy smiling face girl

treatment with stain removal products, though be aware that some fabrics could be damaged by their use. Always proceed with caution where your dolls are concerned.

Eyes

Dolls should always be stored on their fronts so that the eyes stay open. Keeping them on their backs for long periods can cause the eyes to stick shut. Although eye problems can be a sign of 'hard plastic disease' (see relevant section), they are much more likely to be caused by poor storage, or even keeping the doll in a cold room. Although it is tempting to try to open the eyes using fingernails, or even tweezers, it is not really a good idea to try this as the lids can be scratched or the eyes pushed in. Some people suggest using a fine sewing machine oil, but this is not recommended as oil can react with the plastic (resulting in a sticky build-up).

One technique which I have found works in many cases is the use of an eraser. You need a very soft one, of the type used for removing pencil. Ink or typewriter rubbers are much too hard. It is possible to find very narrow pencil erasers shaped like a pencil and these are perfect, but if not, any small, narrow one will suffice. If the doll is very small, hold her securely in one hand, but if she is a larger doll, sit her upright, supported by a cushion. Take the eraser and stroke it gently over the closed lids, attempting to push up the lid. It can be a slow process, but eventually the lids should raise; the eraser often succeeds in gripping the plastic. Keep trying to open and close the lids using the eraser until they work freely.

Lashes

Missing lashes are a very common problem, and are quite straightforward to rectify. The easiest way is to buy a strip of lashes from a stockist of doll repair items or a doll's hospital. Using sharp nail scissors, cut the lash strip to the required length, then apply the tiniest possible amount of white pva glue, using a cocktail stick, along one edge of the strip. Next use tweezers to place the lash strip into position. Often, the strip has to slide into a slot just above the eye, but occasionally it just needs to be stuck along the edge of the lid.

Another way of making lashes is to create a lash strip using an ultra-narrow piece of sticky tape and cutting short lengths of your own hair to place along the strip. However, this is quite fiddly to do, especially with small dolls.

Mohair Wigs

The majority of the earlier 1950s dolls had wigs made from mohair, and this isn't particularly easy to clean and style, though it can be done. I have often come across dolls where attempts have been made to wash the wig in situ. This is not only bad for the doll, as it will inevitably become very wet during the shampooing process, but it also causes the fibres of the wig to matt together into a clump.

If a wig is so filthy that you have no choice, then it is best to remove the wig from the doll and gently swirl it in warm water to clean – only, be aware that it will still clump, and can be extremely difficult to untangle. It can be combed, when dry,

Roddy composition (Never get water on a composition doll)

working from 'root' to tip, but you will probably find that a vast quantity of mohair will fall away during the process.

Normally, it is best to leave mohair alone. Obviously, a really sparse or deteriorating wig can be changed, but try to substitute it with a mohair wig in a similar style to the original. Modern, shiny nylon looks wrong on early hard plastic dolls. Often it is possible to arrange mohair to cover any bald spots, or to put the doll in a bonnet or hat so that she still looks pretty. The hair can then be arranged around the edge, and no one will know unless you remove her bonnet.

One of the most commonly found problems is curl-loss in mohair wigs, but this can be treated quite easily. Depending on the size of doll, wrap strands of hair around pipe-cleaners or pipe-cleaners padded with cloth or tissue, or around rollers intended for humans. Once they are in place, arrange a hairnet over the doll's head to keep the curls in place. Then cover the doll's face with a cloth to protect it, and spray the hair with plain water from a fine plant mister. Take care not to soak the hair, you only need to dampen it slightly. Then leave the hair to dry naturally for a couple of days – please don't be tempted to use a hairdryer. Once dry, remove the pipe-cleaners.

Sometimes, mohair just looks a little flat and unkempt – often a gentle smoothing of the hair, followed by a quick, light spray of water from a plant mister will instantly perk up the wig.

Quick Wigs

It's simplest to buy a wig for a larger doll, but for small dolls it is quite easy to make a basic wig. You will need: a length of mohair, obtainable from a stockist of doll supplies; a length of cotton tape (white for blonde mohair, black or brown for dark mohair), and some white pva glue. Find the necessary length by draping the mohair across the doll's head, and then sew the mohair to the tape by hand (or machine) to form a centre parting. Glue the hair to the head, either all over or just along the centre parting if you prefer, and style. Some people fasten another length of mohair to more tape, gluing it just above the left ear, around the back of the head and to the other ear, before sticking on the other centre parting. This makes for a thicker head of hair. It's really a matter of trial and error and what looks good on one doll, may not suit another.

Other Repairs

Major repairs are probably best left to a doll hospital, but restringing smaller dolls is easy. Very small dolls can have limbs reattached in moments by the simple use of an elastic band or loop of thin round elastic, and a pair of tweezers or a crochet hook. Use the tweezers or hook to push the band through the joint openings in the doll's body, attaching the limbs by their hooks to the band. For slightly larger dolls use round doll-stringing elastic from a doll-making supplier. To thread it, fashion a hook from a piece of wire (an old bicycle spoke is good) making the hook a couple of inches longer than the distance from the doll's hip to shoulder.

Small splits in the seams of hard plastic dolls can sometimes be repaired by holding the split over a steaming kettle, and pushing the edges of the split together, keeping tight hold till the plastic has cooled right down. This should effectively weld the plastic, or reshape it into position so that a thin line of pva glue can be inserted.

Clothing

If you are lucky, your doll will be wearing her original outfit (see Chapter 8 for hints on how to identify it), but it is quite probable that she will be dressed in whatever garment her last little owner chose to put her in. Cotton dresses will look better for a spot of laundering, though be careful with

Pedigree girl doll

reds and strong colours which might run. Wash the clothes by hand using a mild liquid for washing wool. Rinse the garments well, then allow to line dry. Stains can often be removed by rubbing soap into them, leaving for a while, then rinsing. Otherwise use a proprietary stain remover. If the outfit is trimmed with lots of braid or beads, it is best to get it professionally cleaned. This also goes for felt and wool garments.

If your doll needs new outfits, look out for knitting or sewing patterns dating from the 1950s. At doll fairs you will normally find plenty of suitable dresses; also, many talented dressmakers make new dresses from old patterns, using old fabrics, which they sell at the fairs. There are usually beautifully-knitted garments, too. Another possibility is to keep a look out in toyshops, as you may find something suitable amongst the ranges of modern doll's clothes. Often these will be fastened with velcro, but it is easy to remove this and replace with poppers, hooks and eyes or ribbon fastenings, to make them more authentic-looking.

Shoes and socks add a finishing touch – socks can easily be made from tubular finger bandage. Just cut to the length required, measuring from the doll's toe to the middle of the calf, and add a little extra for hems. Gather the fabric at one end, and hem the top edge.

Specialist doll suppliers stock doll's shoes. Most 1950s hard plastic dolls wore plastic Cinderella type shoes (See Chapter 8), usually available from doll fairs.

Linda doll mint with tag

Storage and Display

Damp, excessive heat and prolonged sunlight are particularly damaging to hard plastic dolls. Storing them in a damp loft where air can't circulate properly is asking for trouble (See below). A hard plastic doll kept next to a radiator will eventually begin to craze, and the glue will no doubt dry at the seams, causing them to gape or even to buckle. A doll seated on a window sill in direct sunshine for a long period may well lose most of her colouring. The best place to keep a plastic doll is on a shelf in a frequently used room, in other words one which has air circulating and is at an average temperature. If the doll is regularly handled, this is good too. It makes sure the doll gets turned from time to time, so that if any problems begin to develop, such as fading or limbs working loose, they will be quickly spotted.

Some people like to put a hairnet over mohair wigs to ensure they keep neat (for small dolls, 'bun nets', sold in chemists or hair accessory shops to fit over a chignon, are useful). If a doll looks a little dusty, a whisk with a small feather duster or a soft pastry brush will soon spruce her up; if the wig is really dusty or cobwebby, then place a piece of nylon stocking around the nozzle of a vacuum cleaner, secure with an elastic band, and use it to clean off the dust. The little vacuum cleaners sold for cleaning computers are particularly useful for cleaning dolls.

Hard Plastic Disease – HPD

We don't know for certain what causes HPD; an unstable mix of plastics, maybe. In those early days of the 1950s, manufacturers were constantly experimenting, but as so few of the companies are still in existence, and we don't have records, the cause can't be pinpointed. At the time, plastic was a wonder product, and it's possible that manufacturers were a little too enthusiastic, introducing it without carrying out stringent tests. All we know is that in the early 1990s, collectors became aware of an unwelcome condition affecting certain plastic dolls which eventually made the plastic go into meltdown, causing the dolls to literally disintegrate.

Unfortunately, as the condition was first spotted in *Pedigree* dolls, it was given the name 'Pedigree Doll Disease' (PDD), which put *Pedigree* in a bad light, and was very unfair. When it was realised that the condition could affect other makes of hard plastic doll, the name was changed to 'hard plastic disease' (HPD).

It is important to stress that this condition is relatively rare, and provided certain precautions are taken, the majority of doll collectors will never find the disease amongst their dolls. However, it is important that collectors of hard plastic dolls are aware of the condition and are alert for early symptoms. Provided care is taken with new dolls introduced to the collection, and they are stored correctly, there should be no problems. Some authorities state that the disease is caused by a reaction of metal to plastic, due to rusting of the metal eye pieces or joining rods. Many agree that poor storage conditions are to blame such as storing the doll in a damp loft, warm, moist conditions or wrapped in a plastic bag. High humidity also plays its part.

Symptoms

Frequently, the first indication of HPD is a smell of vinegar, or acetone, a lingering unpleasant smell. Usually, hard plastic has no smell, or just a very faint odour. Further warning signs can be small vertical lines around the nose, roughening around the wrists, noticeable loss of colour (especially in a limb), odd pink or red blotches or the head forming an extreme point, like a Kewpie doll. Another symptom is a pink or red groove appearing across the doll's nose, and which eventually spreads to give a 'pinched' look, as though the doll has caught a cold.

In extreme cases the doll will warp until the whole body appears misshapen. White crusty patches will appear on the surface of the plastic, and then a brown liquid will ooze from the doll; she is literally dissolving. BUT it is important to remember that a crack, red mark or line will not necessarily mean that your doll is going to self-destruct! In the majority of cases these are just symptoms of play, natural stress or ageing.

If, however, you do suspect that your doll has the disease, then it is important to immediately isolate it from any other plastic dolls, because HPD can spread. Detached advisors will tell you to put the doll in the rubbish bin, but this is not an easy thing to do with a treasured doll, which may well be one owned since childhood. Obviously if the doll really smells badly, or was leaking liquid, you would not want to keep it anyway, but if the symptoms are mild, then you could wrap it in tissue or muslin and place in a box, in a different room to your dolls – one that is dry and airy – or even a dry garden shed or garage. HPD only affects dolls made from hard plastic, so vinyl types are fine, although they can attract other problems such as stickiness and colour spots.

Please don't let the faint possibility of HPD stop you from collecting hard plastic dolls. Enjoy them and handle them regularly – dolls that are gently 'played with' are far less likely to suffer than those which stay undisturbed in glass airless cases.

Finally...

Hard plastic dolls were made for a very brief period, just 10 years or so. Yet, during that short time, British manufacturers created beautiful masterpieces, classic designs which have never been bettered. We collectors need to preserve as many different examples as we can. The 1950s gave Britain new hope, filling its people with promise, colour and innovation, and in doing so, also created thousands of exquisite dolls over a short period of time. Now, sadly, Britain has no major doll industry – but, back then, our doll manufacturers reigned supreme!

But that's not all!

Over the last few years, a huge wave of so-called 'Retro' seems to have engulfed not just Britain but America too. Doll designers from many lands have been issuing modern dolls, both fashion and play types, dressed in clothes from the 1950s era. Some of these dolls wear smart, tailored outfits while others celebrate the rock and roll era, in flared poodle-trimmed skirts, tight sweaters or leather jackets. The detail and finish on the outfits is amazing; the dolls are intended for collectors, not for children – a concept which would have been alien back in the 1950s. A novice collector might possibly come across one of these dolls and assume, from its hair style, makeup and clothes, that it hails from the 1950s. It doesn't, it's as modern as tomorrow. However, it certainly isn't a fake, nor a reproduction. It's just an excellent, historical doll, representing the costume of an era. Dolls such as Kitty Collier and Miss America from *Tonner*, the Grease dolls (based on the cult film musical, *Grease*) from *Ashton-Drake* and *Mattel*, and some of the dolls from *Madame Alexander* and *Vogue Ginny*, all wear 1950s outfits. These are, in a way, the kind of dolls we might have been playing with in the 1950s, had the technology (and the money) been around to

Modern Kitty Collier – Tiny Kitty – by Robert Tonner 1950's style

produce them. They reflect the fashions of the day, especially the adult fashions, which most of the 1950s dolls didn't do – the 1950s was still relatively unsophisticated, and our dolls wore cotton frocks, short socks and flat strap shoes. Some of these retro dolls are truly stunning, wearing flared dresses with lots of petticoats, hats and high heeled shoes, or pencil slim skirts and pedal pushers. They have 1950s hairstyles, red lips and, often, a 1950's pout.

Mattel have developed a range of 1950s creations, too, many involving Barbie. As well as the classic 1950s Barbie designs now being reissued, such as her striped swimsuit, there are some featuring 1950s personalities, including Barbie Loves Elvis, which depicts Barbie as an autograph-hunting pony-tailed teen in a pink top and flared black skirt appliqued with Elvis motifs, watching an Elvis doll in a gold lame jacket and black trousers, complete with his guitar. There are also Elvis dolls, The Army Years with Elvis looking smart in his GI uniform, and King of Rock 'n' Roll which has Elvis in his gold lame suit. In Nifty Fifties Barbie looks a typical 1950s teen in her pink flared poodle-decorated skirt, polka dot shirt and black cardigan, while a young Frank Sinatra in his classic 1950s suit is the star of The Recording Years.

Thousands of today's collectors cherish these lovely, modern fashion dolls which hearken back to the 1950s, yet those of us who were children at the time will always prefer the simple, innocent face of a *Pedigree* baby Delite, a *Rosebud* girl or a little *Tudor Rose* baby. It's a nostalgia thing.

Pedigree Saucy Walkers

Where to See Dolls in the UK

Dolls Museum,
Memorial Hall,
High Street,
Dunster,
Minehead
TA24 6SF

Lilliput Doll and Toy Museum
Brading,
Isle Of Wight
PO36 0DJ

Memories of Childhood
Ullapool,
Kyleesku,
Sutherland
IV27 4HW

National Trust Museum of Childhood
Sudbury,
Ashbourne,
Derbyshire
DE6 5HT

Penrhyn Castle
Bangor,
Gwynedd
LL57 4HN

Vina Cooke Museum of Dolls & Bygone Childhood,
The Old Rectory,

Great North Road,
Cromwell,
Newark,
Nottinghamshire
NG23 6JE

V & A Museum of Childhood,
Cambridge Heath Road,
Bethnal Green,
London
E2 9PA

Dolls Hospitals

Bristol Doll and Teddybear Hospital
1 Wycliffe Row,
St Lukes Crescent,
Bristol
BS3 4RU

Crafts Unlimited
5 Scratton Road,
Stanford-Le-Hope,
Essex
SS17 0NZ

Dolls Hospital
Beck House,
Lower St,
Southrepps,
Norwich,
Norfolk
NR11 8UL

Dolly Doctors

The Doll Infirmary,
13 Windsor Road,
Thanington-Without,
Kent
CT1 3UN

Day Dream Dolls
142-144 Middlewich Road,
Winsford,
Cheshire
CW7 3NP

Recollect Dolls Hospital,
17 Junction Road,
Burgess Hill,
West Sussex,
RH15 0HR

Teddy Bear Clinic & Dolls Hospital
The Dolls House,
Stonehall Common,
Kempsey,
Worcester,
Worcestershire
WR5 3QQ

Vina Cooke
The Old Rectory,
Great North Road,
Cromwell,
Newark,
Nottinghamshire
NG23 6JE

Further Reading

A list of books relating to dolls which include details of 1950s companies:

A Collector's Guide to Old Cottage Dolls by Terry and Christine Summers, Summertone Ltd.

British Hard Plastic Dolls Of the 1940s and 1950s by Frances Baird, New Cavendish.

British Toy Business by Kenneth D. Brown, Hambledon Press.

Doll Showcase Looks At Amanda Jane by Susan Brewer, Virtual Valley.

History of The Christmas Fairy Doll by Susan Brewer, Virtual Valley.

Pollock's Dictionary of English Dolls edited by Mary Hillier, Crown.

The Collector's Guide to British Dolls since 1920 by Colette Mansell, Hale.

The Ultimate Doll Book by Caroline Goodfellow, Dorling Kindersley.

Acknowledgements

There isn't room to list everyone who helped out with this book, but grateful thanks to Anne McAndrew, Christine Garner, Margaret Follwell, Wendy Moorhen, Christine Poulten, Jo Birch, Colette Mansell, Frank Strudwick, Terry Summers, Pauline Payne, Doris Howe, Victoria Stevens, Medwyn Owen, Linda Toney, John Mitchell, Joy Beddows, Christine Wimsey, and to all those friends and fellow collectors who gave freely of their knowledge and experience.

Thanks, too, go to my husband Malcolm for his support, to my son Simon for all his technical help and to my daughter Jenna for helping me to sort and research the dolls. Finally, I'd like to pay a special tribute to my late parents, Joan and William Warne – thanks, Mum, for buying my very special composition 'Elizabeth', even though you thought that a nine year old was a bit too old for dolls. And thanks, Dad, for taking all those photos throughout my childhood and so preserving the dolly memories. They have proved very useful.

Picture Credits

Dean's, p98
Joy Beddows, p35 (top left)
Medwyn Owen, p24, 25
Christine Poulten, p30, 31, 32
Terry Summers, p99, 148
Linda Toney, p39 (left)
William Warne, p6, 20, 22, 104, 133, 137, 157

All other photos property of Author.

Index